C000015866

PROFESSIONAL AREA MANAGEMENT
LEADING AT A DISTANCE IN MULTI-UNIT ENTERPRISES

CHRIS EDGER

LIBRI
PUBLISHING

SOME REVIEWS FOR THIS BOOK

A banquet of ideas and techniques for area managers written by the UK's leading multi-site expert…

Paul Charity, Founder and MD, Propel Info
(ranked #2 most influential hospitality journalist in the UK by Allegra)

An invaluable reference guide for those aspiring to be great area managers or those that train/lead them!

Adam Fowle, CEO of Tesco Casual Dining,
Chairman of Giraffe Concepts and NED of Enterprise Inns
(formerly CEO, Mitchells and Butlers Plc and Retail Director,
Sainsbury's)

A great handbook for area managers who wish to improve their professional practice…

Helen Webb, Food Retail Group HRD, The Co-op
(Retail and Distribution HRD, Sainsbury's until 2014)

…the step from unit manager to area manager can be a giant leap… this book can only help newly promoted area managers to make that step more effectively…

Paul Daynes, Group HR Director, St Gobain Building Distribution
(incorporating Jewson, Graham, Gibbs & Dandy etc.)

Another expert book from Professor Edger on area management, that continues his enquiry into this vital retail cadre of managers. This book provides a precise 'how to' guide for area managers without abandoning any of its academic rigour…

Professor Chris Prince, Pro-Vice Chancellor, Leeds Metropolitan
University

...a must have tool for all area managers!

Vanessa Hall, CEO, YO! Sushi
(formerly Operations Director, Premium Estate, Mitchells and Butlers)

...a useful addition to the area manager's armoury... [The] tips and insights in this book can only help area managers to do their jobs more successfully!

Simon Longbottom, recently appointed CEO, Stonegate Pub Co
(previously MD, Greene King PP and MD, Gala Bingo & Casinos)

...New area managers are often given a tablet and a list of units and expected to learn the job through osmosis! This book provides practical tips and insights on how they can do that job more effectively from day one!

Andrew Emmerson, Founder of EDC,
Non-Executive Chairman of Snappy Snaps and NED of Hotcha
(formerly Executive Director Development, Domino's Pizza)

First published in 2014 by Libri Publishing

Copyright © Libri Publishing

The right of Chris Edger to be identified as the author of this work has been asserted in accordance with the Copyright, Designs and Patents Act, 1988.

ISBN 978-1-909818-09-5

All rights reserved. No part of this publication may be reproduced, stored in any retrieval system or transmitted in any form or by any means, electronic, mechanical, photocopying, recording or otherwise, without the prior written permission of the copyright holder for which application should be addressed in the first instance to the publishers. No liability shall be attached to the author, the copyright holder or the publishers for loss or damage of any nature suffered as a result of reliance on the reproduction of any of the contents of this publication or any errors or omissions in its contents.

A CIP catalogue record for this book is available from The British Library

Design by Carnegie Publishing

Cover design by Helen Taylor

Printed by Berforts Information Press

Libri Publishing
Brunel House
Volunteer Way
Faringdon
Oxfordshire
SN7 7YR

Tel: +44 (0)845 873 3837

www.libripublishing.co.uk

CONTENTS

PRACTICES

LIST OF FIGURES AND TABLES

LIST OF ABBREVIATIONS

AM – Area Manager
AVD – Added Value Deviance
B2C – Business to Consumer
BBC – British Broadcasting Corporation
BCBS – Birmingham City Business School
BOH – Back of House
BRAG – Black, Red, Amber and Green (report)
CEO – Chief Executive Officer
COGs – Cost of Goods
COO – Chief Operating Officer
CPI – Continuous Process Improvement
3 Es – Energy, EI and Expertise
EBITDA – Earnings Before Interest Tax Depreciation and Amortisation
EFQM – European Framework for Quality Management
EI – Emotional Intelligence
EMEA – Europe, Middle East and Asia
EPOS – Electronic Point of Sale
ER – Employee Relations
ERP – Enterprise Resource Planning
FOH – Front of House
GM – General Manager
H&S – Healthy and Safety
HIPO – High Potential
HO – Head Office
HQ – Headquarters
HRD – Human Resource Director
HR – Human Resources
HRM – Human Resource Management
IMUE – International Multi-Unit Enterprise
F&B – Food and Beverage
F&F – Fixtures and Fittings
KPI – Key Performance Indicator
KM – Kitchen Manager
LLS – Leisure Leadership and Strategy

M&A – Merger and Acquisition
MD – Managing Director
MNC – Multi-National Corporation
MTQ48 – Mental Toughness Questionnaire
MUE – Multi-Unit Enterprise
MUL – Multi-Unit Leader
MULS – Multi-Unit Leadership and Strategy
MUM – Multi-Unit Manager
NPS – Net Promoter Score
NVQs – National Vocational Qualifications
OPI – Operational and Process Improvement
OTJ – On the Job
OSM – Operational Services Manager
P&L – Profit and Loss
PDF – Practice Distance Fit
PDP – Performance Development Plan
POSE – Portfolio Optimisation through Social Exchange
POV – Point of View
PRP – Performance-Related Pay
QSR – Quick Service Restaurant
RBM – Retail Business Manager
R&T – Recruitment and Training
RM – Regional Manager
ROI – Return on Investment
ROM – Retail Operations Manager
SDT – Store Development Team
SHT – Saville & Holdsworth Test
3 Ss – Service, Systems and Standards
SE – Senior Executive
SET – Social Exchange Theory
SKU – Stock Keeping Unit
SOP – Standard Operating Procedures
SPF – Service Personality Framework
SPH – Spend per Head
SVP – Senior Vice President
TQM – Total Quality Management
UK – United Kingdom
UM – Unit Manager
US – United States
VMT – Visual Merchandising Team
VP – Vice President

ABOUT THE AUTHOR

Professor Chris Edger PhD is the author of *Effective Multi-Unit Leadership – Local Leadership in Multi-Site Situations* (Gower Applied Business Research, 2012) described by the *Leadership and Organization Development Journal* as possibly 'one of the key books of its kind for this decade'. Also the author of *International Multi-Unit Leadership – Developing Local Leaders in International Multi-Site Operations* (Gower Applied Business Research, 2013) and *Franchising – How Both Sides Can Win* (Libri, forthcoming 2015), Chris holds the chair of Multi-Unit Leadership at Birmingham City Business School (BCBS), Birmingham City University, UK. He also teaches at the University of Birmingham and the Warwick Business School, UK, where he is the winner of several teaching excellence awards on the Warwick MBA Programme.

Chris has over twenty years' experience of senior leisure and retail multi-unit operations, sales and support expertise, working for domestic and internationally owned multi-site companies. During his career he has held Area Management and Regional Operations Director positions, including holding responsibility for over 400 units. In addition he has held Executive Board positions as Group Human Resources Director (HRD), Commercial Director and Sales Managing Director in organisations with multi-site interests in China, Eastern Europe and Germany. He has been a member of an Executive Management team that transacted two major cross-border merger and acquisition (M&A) deals that totalled £2.3bn and $1.7bn, respectively.

His specialist teaching areas on the MSc in Multi-Unit Leadership and Strategy at BCBS are Service Leadership and Operational Improvement within retail, hospitality and leisure multi-unit contexts. Chris is also a frequent media commentator, having appeared on or written for outlets such as Channel 4 News, ITV, BBC News Online, InfoDaily, City A.M., Propel Info, Huffington Post, Daily Telegraph.com, the *Retail Gazette, Daily Mail* and *Retail Week*. In addition he provides specialist coaching, training and consultancy advice to a range of multi-unit organisations regarding area management development and performance. He can be contacted at christian.edger@bcu.ac.uk.

Chris has a PhD (ESRC Award, Warwick Business School), MBA and DMS (Nottingham Business School) and an MSc (econ) with distinction (London School of Economics).

ACKNOWLEDGEMENTS*

This 'Area Management' project spanning three books has benefited from the contributions, insights and advice of many people over the past few years; not least **all** the great unit managers and AMs on the BCBS Multi-Unit Leadership and Strategy Programme. I would especially like to thank Paul Charity (Founder and MD, Propel Info), Professor Duncan Angwin (Oxford Brookes University), Emeritus Professor Mike Terry (Warwick University), Professor Chris Brewster (Reading University), Professor Gerald Noone O.B.E. (Newcastle), Martin West (Publishing Editor, Gower), Paul Jervis (Publisher, Libri), Dr Lisa Qixun Siebers (Nottingham Business School, author of *Retail Internationalisation in China*), Liz Phillips (HRD, Mitchells and Butlers), Paul Daynes (Group HRD, St Gobain UK), Adam Fowle (CEO, Tesco Family Dining and Chairman Giraffe Concepts, NED Enterprise Inns), Vanessa Hall (CEO, YO! Sushi), Jan Smallbone (ex-Talent Director EMEA, Starbucks), Ian Burke (Chairman, Rank Plc), Dr Sue Waldock (Group HRD, Rank Plc), Caroline Hollings (HRD, Greene King PP), Reg Sindall (ex-EVP Group Resources, Burberry Plc), Adrian Fawcett (Chairman, Park Holidays, Advest Capital etc.), Joy Levesley (Head of People Development, Marstons), Helen Webb (Group HRD, Co-op Retail), Jerry Robinson (Operations Director, YHA), Mark Taylor (Chief People Officer, Burberry Plc), Michelle Wilkinson (Talent Director, Burberry Plc), Kevin Allcock (National Operations Director, Mecca), Andy Vaughan (ex-Senior Strategy Director, Sodexo), Mark Peters (Talent Director, Spirit), Andrew Emmerson (ex-Development Director, Domino's), Nick Wylde (MD, Stanton Chase International), Kevin Todd (ex-President and CEO, Rosinter Restaurants Russia), Andrew Kitching (Group HRD, Booker Plc), Bryn Thomas (Finance Director, PSA Peugeot Citroen UK), Simon Longbottom (CEO, Stonegate), Dr Nollaig Heffernan (Ecole Hotelier Lausanne), Bob Dignen (CEO, York Associates), James Hyde (Senior Partner, Korn Ferry International), John Woodward (Global CEO, KUE Singapore), Jeremy Townsend (CFO, Rentokil Initial Plc), Mara Swan (EVP Strategy and Talent, ManpowerGroup), Mike Balfour (Founder, Fitness First), Professor Paul Turner (BCBS, ex-SVP HR Convergys), Tim Clarke (Senior NED, ABF Primark), Iain Napier (Chairman,

---

*   Titles and roles correct at time of writing.

Imperial Tobacco; NED, McBride, Grants), Sara Weller (ex-MD, Argos and NED Lloyds Bank, United Utilities), Lee Moody (HRD, Mecca), Clive Chesser (Business Unit Director, Greene King PP), Fiona Gunn (Marketing Director, Wilkos), Peter Blakemore (CEO, Spar Blakemore), Nick Andrews (Operations Director, Mitchells and Butlers), Adam Martin (Customer Services Director, Brakes), David Gallacher (Operations Excellence Director, Yum!), Vicky Quin (Learning and Development Manager, Nando's), John Hegarty (founder, BPA), Deborah Kemp (CEO, Laurel Funerals), Bronagh Kennedy (Company Secretary, Severn Trent) and Alasdair Murdoch (CEO, Gourmet Burger Company).

Lastly (but not least), thank you to my wife and son (Sheenagh and Maxim) for putting up with me writing four books in four years! Also, many thanks to Dr Clinton Bantock, Stephen Willson and Professor Chris Prince for backing me throughout the whole area management project.

A human space is part of the whole called by us universe, a part limited in time and space. We experience ourselves, our thoughts and feelings as something separate from the rest. A kind of optical delusion of consciousness...

Albert Einstein

CHAPTER 1
INTRODUCTION

In developed nations the service sector accounts for nearly two-thirds of GDP, whilst developing/emerging markets are also experiencing a rapid rate of 'economic enfranchisement' which is accelerating their economies towards service-based models. Within these contexts, multi-unit enterprises (MUEs) – otherwise known as chains, multiples or standardised service centres – dominate every aspect of the service industry landscape and are one of the most common organisational forms. However, in spite of their importance there is little research relating to both their organisational form (Garvin and Levesque 2008) and, alarmingly, their key managerial cohorts – area managers (AMs), otherwise known as district or regional operations managers (DiPietro et al. 2007). Sitting between the centre and the local unit, this key cohort of employees occupies a complex and ambiguous position in the organisational hierarchy. On the one hand they are expected by the centre seamlessly to implement strategy and policies within their districts or regions while simultaneously they are faced with a number of counter-pressures emanating from their dispersed portfolio and units. How do they optimise performance in this detached/isolated middle-management space, bedevilled with competing (and sometimes contradictory) interests, claims and demands? How do they optimise performance *at a distance* without being able to exercise direct daily supervision?

This book, based on extensive research into area-management activities, behaviours and characteristics in both developed and developing market contexts during the period 2007–2014, addresses these questions. It is constructed around the central proposition that what effective area managers do to optimise performance – overcoming handicaps of *structural*, *psychological* and *functional distance* (Napier and Ferris 1993) which limit their *interactions* with followers/peers – can be defined as a form of *professional practice*. That is to say that, first, there is convergence between what the best area managers do 'leading at a distance' and, second, this can be represented as a distinctive form of professional conduct that, when defined and scoped, can accelerate the performance of aspirant and extant area managers. Thus this book, having first considered the macro and micro challenges faced by modern-day MUEs and their responses, secondly will describe how area managers optimise *operational excellence* (implementing systems, enforcing standards and executing sales-led service) through *commitment*, *control* and *change*-led practices at portfolio level – which (consciously or unconsciously) they deploy to overcome a myriad of *distance-induced* issues which they face within the archetypal MUE.

THE MULTI-UNIT ENTERPRISE

The multi-unit enterprise is defined as a geographically dispersed organisation built up from *standard* units such as branches, service centres, hotels, restaurants and stores (franchised or managed) which are aggregated into larger geographic groupings such as districts, regions and divisions. These organisations cross many industrial sectors, such as retail banking, clothing, grocery and food retail, hospitality, leisure and services (such as recruitment, pest control, 'office solutions' etc.). Olsen and colleagues provide a useful definition of multi-unit enterprises as organisations that 'compete in an industry with more than one unit of like concept or theme' (1992: 3).

Placing the organisational form in context, there were four inter-related factors that led to the growth of MUEs in developed economies – forces that are currently being mimicked in developing environments. *First*, industrialisation based upon mass production techniques, derived from inventions such as steam-powered machinery, led to a growing urban population which concentrated demand in tight geographical areas. *Second*, the mass production of cheaply priced goods such as food, shoes and clothing opened up broader consumer channels. *Third*, the economic buying power of the new industrialised working classes and urban middle classes (whose real income per head doubled in the late nineteenth century) gave rise to high demand for consumer goods. *Fourth*, the development of sophisticated transport infrastructures revolutionised the supply chain, enabling the transportation of mass-produced goods in bulk to growing urban centres to service this increasing demand.

In terms of operators and sector growth, the earliest multi-unit retailers in the UK were newsagents, such as W H Smith & Son and John Menzies, both of which had established large networks of outlets within and beside railway stations by the 1860s. There then followed two distinct phases in the development of multi-unit enterprises (Jeffreys 1954). Between 1870 and 1890, multiples selling footwear, groceries, meat and household goods spread throughout the UK. From 1890 until 1914, menswear, chemist's and variety store chains followed. These chains adopted strategies which are familiar in the present time, deploying 'economies of scale in buying, economies of specialisation in administration and economies of standardisation in selling' (Jeffreys 1954: 27). By 1900, multiples had 12% of total sales of food and household stores, growing to 20% by 1920. As the growth of motor transport ownership increased and the suburbs extended out from major conurbations, the next innovation, firstly in the US and then in Europe (especially France and the UK), involved large-scale unit development with the introduction of superstores (25,000 square feet) in the 1970s and then hypermarkets (50,000 square feet) in the 1980s. This trend towards scale was copied by other multi-unit retail firms. From the 1960s in the US (and the 1970s in the UK), out-of-town malls and retail parks anchored by food retail, bulky goods and fashion began spreading next to arterial routes near major conurbations. Such developments proved extremely successful in the 1990s and early twenty-first century as consumers, backed by cheap credit and rising incomes, sated their desire for cheap appliances, furniture and clothing. A parallel development, the rise in cheap imports from China, also fuelled consumption at this time as some product categories deflated in price over the period.

With regards to the leisure and hospitality sectors, format standardisation came later than in retail, its emergence being connected to the growth of air and motor transport, the increasing amount of leisure time and rising levels of discretionary spend. In the case of hotels, innovators such as Conrad Hilton in the US began the distribution of upscale standard units with high levels of cleanliness, amenity and service. Mid-scale operators such as Holiday Inn followed, seizing competitive advantage against the variable and fragmented motel sector in the US. In the case of fast food and casual dining, there were entrepreneurs such as Ray Kroc who, having bought the McDonald's concept from the founder in 1956, designed a standard offer that could be duplicated and rolled out in both managed and franchised formats in the US. Throughout the 1960s and 1970s, standardised chains proliferated next to interstate highways and in burgeoning suburbs. These branded operations benefited from adopting many of the 'lean' principles of mass production and modern retailing (Schmenner 1986). Through standardising operations, consolidating the supply chain with bulk ordering and prescribed service delivery systems, these formats, offering consistency and cheap prices, created demand for out-of-home dining which, by 2013, accounted for over half of food consumption in the US. As with retail, the UK followed US trends in hospitality and leisure chain growth. The 1980s saw the swift roll-out of US chains such as McDonald's and Pizza Hut, allied to urban casual dining inventions such as PizzaExpress. Today, Quick Service Restaurants (QSR) and fast casual concepts are proliferating rapidly within the UK market, driving out-of-home dining expenditure on 'small treat' occasions to unprecedented levels. Today a major trend in this sector (and to a large extent in retail) is the proliferation of different brand formats and a high degree of local product customisation to address specific micro-market demand.

THE OPERATIONAL CORE

One major feature of MUEs is their *physical dispersion* (i.e. centre to unit) resulting in the operational line playing a vital role in ensuring 'implementation'. Typically, there are four levels of manager that sit in this area, fulfilling strategic and non-strategic roles according to their levels of seniority: divisional director, regional director, area manager and unit manager. In the view of Garvin and Levesque, who refer to these managers as 'the field', this cohort is key:

> the success of the multiunit corporation depends on the competence, capabilities and commitment of field managers, who embody the brand through their actions, oversee daily operations, and implement new initiatives…

> (Garvin and Levesque 2008: 6)

What is significant about these roles is the degree to which, first, unlike other business structures, the operational core has a high degree of *mutually interdependent accountabilities* and responsibilities to create a 'multi-layered net' that is designed to prevent operational breakdowns caused by spatial detachment (Garvin and Levesque 2008). Second, their jobs are less specialised than those of middle managers in classic bureaucratic organisations, having a set of general management functions which involve the supervision of standards, systems and service (see Chapter 3).

As previously stated, it is the contention of this book that the key role in the operational hierarchy – indeed throughout multi-unit organisations – is the area manager (AM). Indeed in Garvin and Levesque's 'model of overlapping responsibilities' (2008: 5), *eight out of the ten fundamental priorities* of the operational line fall within the AM domain, a far higher number than for the three other operational management cohorts (unit, regional and divisional).

THE AREA MANAGER

But where does the origin of the AM role lie and what does previous research tell us about its key duties and responsibilities?

HISTORY

An AM – also called an Area Coach, District Manager, Regional Manager, Retail Operations Manager, Retail Business Manager or Business Development Manager – is the key interface between the centre and units in managed and/or franchised branded multi-site enterprises – MUEs. In 'developed' markets, as MUEs and more layers of senior management were created in the late nineteenth century, the hierarchy of larger chains mimicked the command structure of mechanistic and bureaucratic forms of manufacturing organisations. At first, in the absence of central technology, these managers assumed a policing role at unit level, being titled 'agents', 'store supervisors' and 'store inspectors' (Mathias 1967). As businesses developed paper-based stock taking, pricing, merchandising and ledger systems, these 'inspectors' ensured that units were run professionally and consistently according to company policy. One major innovation that brought the importance of AMs into sharper focus was the growth of franchise retail in 'developed' markets in the late 1960s. For instance, in the US it is believed that a significant mediating factor in the proliferation of fast-food offerings was the AM, although observers have noted how little is known about their early duties, responsibilities and impact (Ritzer 1993). However, given the systemisation of food production and strict franchising rules, some research has indicated that they played a pivotal role in ensuring consistency of standards and execution (Umbreit and Smith 1991).

PREVIOUS RESEARCH

With regards to generic AM research, a full elaboration of the literature is contained in my first book on the subject (Edger 2012: 22–8). The main points contained within this literature – which is almost entirely based on studies conducted with the US fast-food industry – is that academics believe that there are a number of critical success factors or job dimensions pertaining to the role and, moreover, there are certain managerial practices which, if applied, can result in more effective performance. With regard to the former – the vital components of the role – Umbreit's ground-breaking analysis established that there were five critical dimensions: *operations*, *financial management*, *HRM*, *marketing and promotions management*, and *facilities and safety* (Umbreit 1989). Further studies sought to test the relative importance and hierarchy of these aspects, concluding that operations and HRM were deemed to be the most important job attributes, followed by financial management, marketing and safety (Umbreit 1989, Mone and Umbreit 1989, Umbreit and Smith 1991, Ryan 1992, Muller and Campbell 1995, Reynolds 2000). Repeating Umbreit's study, little divergence from these findings was found either within a care-home context (Brzezicki 2008) or in the UK pub industry (Jones and Inkinci 2001).

These and further texts also considered the transitional difficulties that unit managers encountered moving into AM roles; the major issues relating less to technical issues (due to their previous unit manager experience) but rather to those of HRM and leadership caused by managing 'remotely at a distance' (Umbreit 1989, DiPietro et al. 2007, Rivera et al. 2008). Stress, tension and quit rates within this cohort were found to correlate positively to a lack of HRM skills and the burdensome demands of the job (Umbreit 1989, Ryan 1992). In order to be successful, MUMs had to learn to delegate key functions and activities across their areas in order to 'de-stress' the role, learning to 'manage the managers' rather than seek to 'manage every unit' and create and leverage broader support networks within the organisation (Umbreit and Smith 1991, BHI 2005a, b).

Continuing these important studies, I undertook a major research project from 2007 to 2012 which sought to devise an integrated model of effective multi-unit leadership (Edger 2012). It departed from previous research in that it extended across multi-unit sectors (i.e. retail, leisure and hospitality); triangulated the views of senior operators, AMs and unit managers (from both 'owner' managed and multiple franchise 'chain within a chain' perspectives); and attempted to devise a guiding framework that captured the key activities, behaviours and characteristics of effective AMs. The major insight provided by this study was that a guiding theory applied to this domain, namely portfolio optimisation through social exchange (POSE). That is to say that, due to their high levels of interdependence with their followers juxtaposed with *'distance'* issues, coupled with the fact that each of their units differed to some degree (i.e. location, site layout, serviceable market, labour access etc.), AMs could be conceived of as *local leaders*, optimising their portfolios (areas and districts) by exercising *local HRM* – transacting emotional, social and practical HRM *'currency exchanges'* which could be subdivided into four main categories with sub-components:

- **Mutual goal attainment**
  - local direction setting and prioritisation
  - ability to influence
- **Free market exchange**
  - positional patronage
  - protection from punishment
  - promissory speed
  - permission to innovate
  - scarce resource access
- **Compensated costs**
  - public recognition
  - granting of autonomy
  - emotional capital
  - 'treats'
  - portable skills
  - behavioural coaching
- **Uncovering hidden value**
  - knowledge transfer
  - valuable insights.

Figure 1.1 Effective MUL 'Currencies of Exchange'
(Edger 2012: 250–61)

I also found that, in addition to transacting vertically, effective AMs did so horizontally with colleagues (through 'tangible and intangible asset swaps') and support staff (through empathy, recognition and execution). They also actively encouraged 'inter-unit reciprocity' between units or within 'clusters' and/or geographical 'families' where hard and soft exchanges were made to benefit the portfolio as a whole. The study concluded that:

> **Given the distance** of the AM from their sites, their high level of interdependency with their followers and the ambiguities and complexities of operating in an (often) chaotic and disorderly multi-unit context, it is the effective AM's [local leadership] ability to *exchange social, emotional and practical currencies* both horizontally and vertically – encouraging *value-added reciprocation* from his/her followers, peers and other providers – that marks them out as outstanding *local leaders…*

> (Edger 2012: 268)

The issue with this study is its almost exclusive concentration on AM practice within 'developed' markets such as the UK and US. Therefore, in my next book (Edger 2013) I addressed the conundrums faced by international MUEs in developing effective multi-unit leader cohorts in cultural contexts which featured high levels of self-protective leadership (which militated against Western notions of participative/emancipative leadership) and collectivism (which worked against personal initiative, accepting 'outsiders' and 'owning up' due to 'loss of face'). It was found that in order to be successful in developing a high performance cadre of AMs, international MUEs had to ensure that their organisational values transcended contrarian local mores through intensive immersion, education, conditioning and modelling.

DISTANCE LITERATURE

One issue that resonated in my first two books – confirming the observations of scholars that had previously studied this cohort (Umbreit 1989, DiPietro et al. 2007) – was that of *distance*. As stated, the way in which I found that AMs had dealt with this was through *exchanging* practical, social and emotional currencies that 'bound followers in', ensuring that they could 'lead without direct supervision'. What was missing from the accounts in these books, however, was a proper conceptualisation of leader–member distance (Bligh and Riggio 2013, Schyns 2013). This was a major omission, given the assistance it could have provided us in understanding how it had been previously been framed and researched by previous scholars.

In fact, leader–follower distance has been a major source of enquiry since the early twentieth century, with many states and forms of detachment having been located by scholars operating in this domain: spatial (Simmel 1908), social class and race (Park 1924), personal (Poole 1927), material, psychological, social and cultural (Rummel 1976). One framework that has been frequently used as a proxy for distance measurement is the three-dimensional model proposed by Napier and Ferris (1993):

- **Structural**: Comprises both spatial geographical/physical distance (affecting spans of control and the frequency of personal interaction with others) and hierarchical layers (mediating organisation, supervision and alignment)
- **Psychological**: Includes perceived similarities between leaders and followers framed by factors such as demographics, culture/values, power, ideology, status, goals, mood, personality and so forth
- **Functional**: Encompasses perceptual congruence between parties and the quality of relationships between 'insider' and 'outsider' groups within organisations.

Further research by academics such as Antonakis and Atwater (2002) reframed this three-dimensional model to incorporate social distance, physical distance and perceived interaction frequency, introducing the concept of the 'proximal leader' who maintains a low physical distance with a high frequency of interaction.

But what are the pros and cons of leader–member distance? Distance can work to the advantage of leaders in a variety of ways, such as by preventing 'over-familiarity' (thereby preserving a 'clean image' and a degree of mystery) or by granting time and space to take a broader perspective and recharge depleted energy levels (Shamir 1995). Indeed, in large modern organisations (particularly those with multi-site configurations), since leaders are likely to be situated in different locations from their followers, it is impossible for them to reduce social distance – a distinct benefit perhaps when (s)he has to take tough or unpalatable decisions. From a follower perspective there are also benefits to distance from leader 'interference', including (potentially) greater autonomy, higher levels of intrinsic motivation (caused by the absence of direct daily supervision) and the capacity to express high levels of individuality and form powerful sub-cultures with a binding sense of identity (Collinson 2005).

Overall, however, excessive leader–member detachment is seen as negative and dysfunctional by most academics as it results in diminished levels of trust and – due to the leader's distance from daily operations – strategic policy/practice-making imprecision. So what are the practical solutions for distant leaders?

- **Structural** – Perceived physically distant leaders should:
  - Get to know their team members' capabilities/goals (Zhu et al. 2009)
  - Involve employees in decision making (Shirom 2006)
  - Get people involved in interesting projects (May et al. 2004)
  - Utilise power of self-managed teams
- **Psychological** – Perceived socially/demographically/culturally distant leaders should:
  - Create a culture of high engagement (Corace 2007) and perceived supervisor support through:
    - a sense of direction
    - investment in training and development
    - creation of a trusting environment (lack of 'reprisals')
    - sanctioning of autonomy
    - steady flow of information/communication (openness)
  - Achieve a good person–job fit
- **Functional** – Perceived functionally distant leaders should:
  - Encourage 'insider' interactions with 'outsiders'
  - Personally engage in (job-relevant) refreshment and training

BOOK PURPOSE AND STRUCTURE

As previously stated, this book which addresses the *professional practice* of AMs is born out of the insights and research for *this* and my previous two books that addressed the 'art and science' of AMs in both developed and emerging markets (Edger 2012, 2013). All of these books are based upon in-depth research (2007–2014) comprising:

- **Primary Research (Figure 1.2)**

Method	Level*	Sectors*	Co*	N*
Focus Groups	UM, AM	R, H, L	12	416
Semi-Structured Int.	UM, AM, SE	R, H, L	21	163
Engagement Surveys	UM	H	2	2,627
Accompanied Visits	AM, SE	R, H, L	16	35
Psychometric Testing	AM, UM	R, H, L	8	342
Expert Interviews (IMUE book)	SE, AC, CON	R, H, S	21	–

Level: UM (Unit Managers), AM (Area Manager), SE (Senior Executive), AC (Academic), CON (Consultant); **Sectors**: R (retail), H (hospitality), L (leisure), S (service); **Co**: companies; **N**: numbers of participants

- **Secondary Research**
  - Participant Observer: During 1995–1997, the author was Commercial Director for a UK leisure Corporation, over-seeing the franchised entry of two US leisure brands into the UK market (Dave and Buster's and Wendy's). From 1997 to 2002, the author operated as a parent company executive in an MNC organisation (turnover £2 billion, EBITDA of £220 million and 10,000 employees) with a wholly owned business in the Czech Republic (3,000 employees) and a joint venture in China (2,500 employees). Until 2010, the author was Group HR, Service and Productivity Director of the largest casual dining chain in the UK which also owned a multi-unit hospitality business in Germany.
  - Documents: AM job descriptions and competency models, AM training and development material, AM communications and briefs, company, regional, brand, district and unit KPIs and balanced scorecards, operational manuals etc.

Leveraging the research underpinning three books (including this one), this enquiry, *first*, goes a step further *in its level of analysis* than its predecessors by addressing the following questions:

- How do MUEs typically seek to reduce distance between 'the centre' and the units?

- What are the common 'detachment issues' that continue to persist in MUEs?
- What techniques, mechanisms and interventions do AMs deploy to close down structural, psychological and functional forms of distance within MUEs?

Second, this book seeks to strip back some of the 'academese' of the previous two books and is intended to provide a more pithy *'how to'* guide, with questions at the end of the sections in chapters 4–7 that AMs (and their developers) can reflect upon and use in day-to-day situations to overcome the various dimensions of distance in order to drive portfolio performance.

In order to address the central enquiries of this endeavour, the book is constructed around the following questions:

- Chapter 2: MUE Challenges and Responses

  As a precursor to considering the professional practice of AMs, consideration of context is required: what are the 'macro'/'micro' challenges that face MUEs at the present time and what have been their responses? To what extent are these organisation-level responses designed to reduce the main dimensions of distance?

- Chapter 3: Operational Excellence

  How do organisations conceive of and measure the AM role? This chapter will consider the three principal aspects of operational excellence – systems, standards and sales-led service – followed by the issues AMs face in expediting their duties. To what extent do the issues they face actually increase the dangers of detachment and a lack of capacity to act?

- Chapter 4: Commitment

  What local leadership practices do AMs deploy to generate commitment and discretionary effort? To what particular aspects of the distance typologies – outlined in 'Distance Literature' above – do they conform?

- Chapter 5: Control

  How do AMs exert operational grip, assuring defined outcomes through mastery, planning and organisation? To which aspects of the distance typologies – outlined in 'Distance Literature' above – do they conform?

- Chapter 6: Change

  How do AMs ensure brand/site evolution/'fit' through a number of pertinent change-led interventions? To which aspects of the distance typologies – outlined in 'Distance Literature' above – do they conform?

- Chapter 7: Characteristics and Development

  What are the five key attributes that underpin effective AMs? Which attributes are most pertinent to closing down each distance variant?

- Chapter 8: Conclusions

  How can we reframe our notions and understanding of AMs and distance? Can we construct a table that encapsulates AM practice–distance fit (PDF)?

MUE CHALLENGES AND RESPONSES

As a precursor to outlining 'operational excellence' and the professional practice of effective area managers (leading and managing at a distance), consideration must be given to organisation-level challenges and responses within the multi-unit enterprise (MUE) universe which affect the AM role. For sure, from an organisational point of view, due to considerations relating to external environmental and internal organisational factors, the area manager is faced with a plethora of issues and challenges in MUEs (for a complete overview, see Edger 2012 and Edger 2013)! *First*, from a *macro* environmental point of view, the role of an AM is heavily affected by mediating factors such as the national/regional business system, national culture and sector, coupled with disruptive forces relating to economics, technological innovation and changing consumer preferences. *Second*, with regards to the *micro* organisational context, factors which have an impact on the AM role include idiosyncratic features relating to the MUE organisational form. *Third*, these macro and micro pressures can be ameliorated – and the job of the AM made far easier – if the *responses* of senior policy makers (i.e. strategy, culture and architecture) are pertinent to the challenges faced.

'MACRO' ENVIRONMENTAL CHALLENGES

'Macro' external environmental factors which provide challenges for the successful execution of the area manager role in MUEs include:

   a. **National business system** (i.e. laws, officialdom, unions and customs): In liberal/democratic developed territories, where laws relating to employment, health & safety (H&S) and planning are relatively transparent, the auditing/compliance aspect of the AM role can be codified. In developing/emerging territories where legal systems might be more opaque, with officialdom exerting a strong local 'influence', AMs – often called 'city managers' in order to 'match' the level of the officials with whom they are dealing – might be called upon to 'smooth the path' of developments and permit renewals through what might speciously be called 'gifting'. In addition, depending upon the strength of organised labour and regional customs, AMs will act as mediators/trouble-shooters with union representatives and customs officials.

b. **National culture** (i.e. norms, values and customs): In developed contexts where there is a (general) acceptance of participative and emancipative values, MUEs can propagate 'Western' leadership approaches encompassing involvement, empowerment, autonomous team working, two-way communication and so forth. This eases the function of AMs attempting to manage at a distance because at least (in theory) their unit managers will assume accountability and demonstrate initiative. In developing/emerging markets which have had recent experience of central command economies and authoritarian leadership regimes, cultures are apt to display attributes such as high power distance, 'in group' collectivism, excessive uncertainty-avoidance and highly diffuse behaviours manifesting themselves in displays of self-protective leadership, 'master–servant' behaviour, communications on a 'need to know' basis and a lack of meaningful workplace engagement (House et al. 2004). Although increasing wealth, education and access to information through digitalisation is changing some of these values, the issue that arises for AMs is how (particularly in international MUEs) they can apply 'Western' organisational values in cultures where people are programmed to think and behave in contrarian ways. In particular, how can AMs – managing at a distance – be assured that their charges adhere to the 'company way of doing things', resolve problems independently at source and speak up when things have gone awry (i.e. avoid covering up)?

c. **Sectoral image**: Sectors such as hospitality, leisure and retail, which account for a large proportion of service-based MUEs, suffer from idiosyncratic issues that pose particular problems for AMs whatever the context – developed or developing market. Excepting 'high-end' premium products, such sectors suffer from a poor image due to low rates of entry pay, lack of professional status and indeterminate craft/technical training. In developing contexts, in particular, the most highly valued jobs reside in the government or professions. Indeed, retail and hospitality are largely characterised by having high levels of 'transitional' workers (migrants, young people and part-timers) and, therefore – relative to other sectors – high rates of labour turnover. The challenge for the AM is to maintain consistency and dependability at unit level through co-opting and motivating stable management teams that can cope with regular changes in personnel.

d. **Disruptive forces**: In my first two books, I also outlined a 'holy trinity' of disruptive forces that confronted MUEs from the late 'noughties', which continue to resonate at the time of this book's publication:

- *Macro-economic*: In developed market contexts, the recent stalling/collapse of GDP in some territories, due to a banking crisis brought about by unsustainable asset bubbles and unsupportable welfare/benefit structures, led to many MUEs scaling back their investment programmes and 'delayering' staff levels in response to falls in consumer discretionary spend. Thus, AMs have had to manage (in some cases) savage labour and benefit reduction programmes whilst attempting to maintain the integrity of their product responsi-bilities. In some developing/emerging contexts, the opposite has applied with exponential growth rates creating a demand for skilled labour that is in scarce supply. In such contexts a 'war for talent' has ensued with AMs fighting to hang onto their best GMs and line leadership.

- *Technological/digital*: A revolution brought about by the Internet and portable 'smart' technology devices has heralded a shift in the way in which people browse, order, purchase and collect products. In the retail sector, MUEs that have *not* adopted a multi/omni-channel approach are threatened with extinction, whilst many MUEs that have retailed in catego-ries that have been commoditised by digital channels (i.e. books, electrical, white goods, music and video) have gone into administration. Although some innovations such as 'click and collect' have deferred some of the cost of channel shifts (with the consumer having to do the pick-up themselves) and the installation of self-service checkout devices reducing labour overhead, retailers are still adapting their systems and processes to fit the new digital paradigm. In hospitality, the Internet has brought greater transparency of quality, choice and price, with couponing/discounts becoming a ubiquitous means of attracting traffic (particularly to fill non-peak occasions). Such changes have increased the pressures on AMs to become more adaptive and innovative within their portfolio of units, rapidly taking on board systems and process changes but also thinking more imaginatively and creatively as to how they can capture trade in their local micro-markets. Also, as digital innovation has made the transmission of 'real-time' information by organisations/agencies easier, such immediacy has posed issues for AMs who, lacking direct control for the structured flow of communications, can be placed 'behind the curve' with their people – a situation which undermines their credibility/authority.

- *Customer preferences*: In developed contexts due to the aforementioned economic issues which have resulted in higher levels of unemployment, wage freezes and general feelings of insecurity/uncertainty, there has been a pronounced consumer drift – within retail in particular – towards a requirement for quality *and* value. The ramifications of this have been moves – certainly within supermarket retail – to extend product ranges to 'good' (i.e. value), 'better' (i.e. mid) and 'best' (i.e. premium). Value operators such as 'dime stores' that have been able to source quality branded products – albeit in smaller stock keeping units (SKUs) – have fared particularly well challenging 'mid-market' retail business models. In developing contexts, an economically enfranchised growing middle class with exponentially growing consumptive capacity has demonstrated a strong appetite for 'status' premium products and hospitality brands that offer quality assurance. The implication for area managers, on both counts, is that they have to keep pace with the changing aspirations and behaviours of their customers.

'MICRO' ORGANISATIONAL CHALLENGES

Internal organisational factors – which are largely idiosyncratic to the multi-unit form – provide challenges for the successful execution of the AM role in MUEs and include:

- *Consistency and uniformity*: Given the number of units in multi-unit organisations and their wide geographical spread, problems of time, distance and space constantly threaten consistency and dependability of the offer (Olsen et al. 1992). Ensuring uniformity is difficult given the remote nature of the units and, in spite of technology and physical infrastructure, its dependence on human execution makes it susceptible to quality, service and standards breakdowns. Spatial and span of control issues are the enemies of the coordination of standardised product quality and service. Consumers experiencing variable and indeterminate quality across a range of, supposedly, standard units are unlikely to trust the offer, leading to high levels of non-repeat business and low net promoter scores.

- *Standardisation versus customisation*: In spite of this drive for consistency, one of the myths of the multi-unit is that all firms impose total operational standardisation. Factors such as non-standard unit footprints (due to site availability constraints), regional tastes and customs, customer demographics, levels of ambient competition and differing local labour markets all impinge upon the operations of single-site units. It should be understood that, in effect, each unit within a multi-unit portfolio operates within its own local micro-market, in which multi-unit firms often make an effort to customise their operations in order to maximise revenues. Some firms operate according to a principle of fixing perhaps 80% of their operations, allowing the other 20% to vary according to local needs. This tension between conformity and flexibility is a constant problem within the multi-unit model, with the centre favouring uniformity (and therefore certainty) and with the unit arguing for greater operational latitude with regards to wages, layout, promotional offer and range. The dangers of increased customisation are obvious – complexity, sub-optimal decision making and (potentially) increased cost – threatening the very premises upon which multiples were founded, namely: consistency and efficiency.

- *Format and channel proliferation*: Multi-unit enterprises have a propensity, either organically or through acquisition, to develop new brands, formats or channels. Constant refreshment, innovation and adaptation are necessary in order to meet changing demands and requirements. Acquiring and/or developing new brands/formats or opening up additional multi-channel routes to market, as an adjunct to existing offerings, however, are problematic for the extant estate, which might be threatened with capital and knowledge starvation to fund new ventures. In the case of new format development within existing brands, several format types (such as smaller 'micro click and collect' sites) can proliferate within any given chain, making the operation of the enterprise complicated. Also, given the vital importance of *location* to site performance, multi-unit chains will often designate units 'core' and 'non-core', leading to twin-track capital and people investment programmes. Again this is problematic to both consumers – who will notice inconsistency – and unit staff in the 'non-core' units who feel like victims of an informal class system: neglected and under threat, resenting their lack of access to resources in comparison to 'higher caste' members within the system. Thus, constant brand development, format extension and/or site acquisitions, coupled with changing external micro-market dynamics, create a high degree of complexity within the portfolio for both policy makers and the operational line. How do policy makers adapt their offers to a 'two-speed' estate? How does the operational line manage new multi-channel innovation alongside existing operations? Often, firms will react to the changes in their estate profiling by re-shaping operational geographies and responsibilities (usually at the beginning of financial years) in order to focus effort. Whilst rational from an organisational point of view, constant boundary revisions are extremely disruptive to relationships within the operational line.

- *Centre-versus-local tensions*: One significant aspect of multi-unit enterprises is the existence of boundary tension and conflict between centrally based functions (such as marketing, HR, audit and supply chain) and field-based operations. On paper, the centre dictates strategy, pricing, promotions, policies and positioning whilst the field-based operation busies itself with flawless implementation. In practice, however, major issues arise when dislocations occur in communication and consultation with the operators on new guidance, initiatives or projects. A lack of information transmission both upwards and downwards through the enterprise due to the dispersion of units is a serious rate limiter in multi-unit enterprises. In firms where a lack of coordination exists at the centre and/or the firm is reacting quickly to regulatory or competitive pressures, constant requests for information and new dictats can seriously disrupt the operational rhythm of the business. Customer-facing operators can be distracted by endless bureaucracy and administrative compliance rather than providing great quality service. The introduction of new technology over the last fifteen years, which has enabled the centre to communicate with units in real time, might have given the centre the illusion that it has more control when, in actual fact, its constant stream of requests and changes to procedure create anxiety, stress and despondency at unit level resulting in reduced levels of commitment and discretionary effort.

ORGANISATIONAL RESPONSES

MUEs are not inert bodies governed by the laws of pre-determination. In response to many of the macro and micro challenges above, policy makers have options they can choose among to ameliorate/overcome extant issues. Elucidating a full range of responses is not possible within the confines of this book (instead, see Edger 2012). However – pertinent to the enquiry of this book (leading at a distance in multi-site enterprises) – there are three responses (strategic, cultural and structural) that will certainly mitigate some of the challenges outlined in the sections above.

a. **Strategy and business model**: Successful strategies typically possess a number of key attributes. *First*, they are constructed around a *'big idea'* relating to what the MUE exists for, what it is trying to do and how it is going to do it (i.e. vision, mission/purpose and tactics). *Second*, it meets a distinctive consumer need, has sufficient separation from that of its competitive set – carving out a degree of 'white space' (through 'exciter' attributes) – and is well communicated/understood by staff and customers. *Third*, this *distinctiveness* – whether it lies within low cost, differentiated or value-based paradigms – is constantly evolved by policy makers as competitors attempt to imitate or 'catch up'. To this extent policy makers are 'ahead' of the service life-cycle curve in anticipating and planning interventions (such as acquisitions and design/product changes) that head off maturity/decline. *Fourth*, the underlying business model (i.e. the end-to-end value chain) is melded to the MUE's strategy. In least-cost business models where a 'lean' philosophy might prevail, it is important that multiple interlocking processes are designed around the principles of economy. Premium business models are generally constructed around end-to-end levels of quality, amenity and service. Often aspects of the business model can incorporate different routes to market, through multi-branding, format variations and/or a multiplicity of ownership models seeking to increase control or mitigate capital exposure/risk (i.e. directly managed, franchised, licensed or concessions).

In MUEs that provide this degree of strategic clarity and business model coherence, the job of the AM in generating followership and buy-in is made easy. However, all too often, AMs will be coping to survive in companies that pursue indistinct strategies that are poorly communicated/evolved, with a supporting business model that is unfit for purpose. Undoubtedly, one of the main contingent factors that can mitigate strategic drift is the quality of the senior leadership cadre of the MUE.

Case Study 1: Responding to Disruption in 'Big Box' Supermarket Retail

Written by the author, this article was cited/published in Channel 4 News online, BBC News online and the Retail Gazette *in April 2013.*

From the 1990s onwards, the received orthodoxy in UK supermarket retail was that 'bigger' meant 'better'. In a 'race for space', operators such as Tesco and Asda opened hundreds of square footage per annum – largely edge-of-town hypermarkets – in which they were able to expand their ranges into non-food categories such as electrical, audio, books, clothing etc. At the time, the winners were perceived to be those that sunk capital into new out-of-town sites and/or extended their existing space (through mezzanines and 'bolt-ons'). This strategy was fine as long as companies could sweat these large expensive assets, optimising sales through constant range and product extensions. However, the onset of Internet trading, which has commoditised or cannibalised many of these non-food categories, has rendered a lot of this space redundant. Over the last three years, **item sales** in these hypermarkets have declined by approximately 2% per annum, with (in some cases) only food price inflation and expansion into the convenience sector propping

CONTINUED ...

up organisational like-for-like sales comparisons. The question that many of the operators of these 'retail cathedrals' surrounded by a 'sea of car parking' face is how they are going to utilise their larger assets more effectively given current consumer trends.

The purchase of the 'better' family urban casual dining concept Giraffe by Tesco this week (approximately 50 sites purchased for a consideration of £50m) – alongside their investment in 'best' coffee concept Harris + Hoole – gives us some indication as to where the supermarket behemoths are heading in this regard. The 'eating out' restaurant and casual dining market in the UK has fared better than retail during the recent downturn (performing at 3–4% annual growth), with consumers still prepared to deploy their discretionary spend on 'small treat' occasions. 'Retailtainment' malls such as Westfield, Merry Hill, Trafford Centre and Meadowhall have had few problems finding tenants for their 'food courts'. Consumers seem very keen to combine retail therapy with gastronomic indulgence! Can Tesco achieve the same?

For sure, the provision of better food service offers might better utilise hypermarket 'dead space', attracting greater footfall and encouraging longer dwell times. Other offers that will be engineered into this space over time might include upmarket concessions, services (health and beauty), pop-up market traders etc. Such moves would increase the atmospheric dynamic of visiting hitherto functional environments. However, this dramatic increase in variety in supermarket retailing threatens to disrupt the very factors that led to organisational success in the first place – huge volumes underpinned by lean supply and service systems. Going beyond the simplicity of volume and value means encountering (and dealing with) the complexity of variety and ensuring quality over a range of unfamiliar products/services. In the case of Tesco, the investment in 'emotional' products/services that will fill space, whilst simulta-neously increasing the 'personality' of its brand and sites, seems to be a sensible move. Tesco's success will rest on whether their business model will cope with greater 'emotional' complexity rather than fighting purely on value/price to drive footfall. The jury is out…

THREE KEY 'STRATEGY AND BUSINESS MODEL' QUESTIONS FOR MUE DECISION MAKERS

1. Do you have an 'elevator pitch' business model (i.e. one that is easy to explain/understand for all stakeholders)?

2. If, in response to competitive forces, you are changing the business model, are you sure it addresses a *real* (rather than perceived!) consumer need? Does it increase simplicity or increase complexity? (The former is preferable to the latter!)

3. Also, do you have the appropriate operational resources/ capabilities to execute any proposed modifications that might profoundly change the way in which you do business?

b. **Senior leadership and culture**: What styles and approaches do effective senior leaders within MUEs require to craft a successful strategy and co-opt strong followership? According to the firm life cycle concept, the types of leadership style required during start-up, rationalisation, accelerated roll-out and maturity differ (Reynolds et al. 2007). Fluid, 'laissez-faire' and organic styles allied with systems of 'soft' HRM are required in the early stages of development, in contrast to the mechanistic and 'autocratic' leadership style melded with a 'hard' HRM approach required during maturity. Often, following concept development and initial roll-out, visionary pioneer-leaders require replacement by rational professional managers who have the skills to leverage MUE scale efficiency. However, problems occur when this administrative cadre is faced with major discontinuities that threaten the enterprise's business model. Their default style of standardised 'compliance and control' leadership is insufficiently agile/flexible to deal with fast-changing external environments as they are locked into outmoded thought patterns suited to old, rather than new, paradigms. They lack the imagination and ingenuity to galvanise their 'inert, ossified' organisations around a 'big idea' that is a clear point of market difference, clearly understood by internal and external stakeholders. Clearly, senior leaders need to be equipped through personality and capability (technical, behavioural and cognitive) to overcome such deter-minism, displaying adaptability, versatility and agility to respond effectively to situational factors.

Inevitably, the *culture* of the MUE will be strongly influenced by the personality and styles of the senior leadership cadre who, themselves, have been imprinted and socialised by the values of their country of origin. Archetypal organisational cultures (i.e. shared motives, values, beliefs, identities and interpretations) have been classified as incorporating four types – power, role, task/achievement and person/support (Harrison 1972) – which is then reflected in the degree to which organisations display preferences for/against innovation and risk taking, attention to detail, outcome/people/team orientation, stability and aggressiveness. However, the main issue that senior leaders have in MUEs (as elsewhere!) is that of change. The wrong culture (i.e. stability) might be confronting a new commercial reality (i.e. technological disruption). How do they galvanise the organisation to adopt new ways of thinking and behaviour? Within such a context, the role of the AM is critical in adjusting the mindsets and disposition of their followers. What will help, however, is if the functional elements of the firm – its architecture and processes – are set up effectively.

c. **Architecture and process**: MUE organisational form is determined by external issues such as market complexity (product, geography and customer) and internal factors such as firm-life, professional elites and culture/ideology. MUEs are generally designed around six building blocks: the strategic apex, technostructure, support staff, ideology, middle line and operating core. The dominance of any of these building blocks is contingent on factors such as the level of supervision required, degree of standardisation of work, skills, outputs or norms. In terms of architecture, common forms include simple, machine bureaucracy, professional bureaucracy, divisionalised adhocracy and missionary (Mintzberg 1979), which are configured according to situational factors (i.e. multi-brand and/or international) and key design parameters. But given the standardised nature of the product and outputs of MUEs (due to the need for economic efficiency through replication), what key architectural design characteristics do MUEs display to ensure the smooth running of operations?

- *Alignment mechanisms*: Unlike many other organisational forms, operational roles within multi-unit enterprises are general rather than specialised. This means that accountability and responsibility for many metrics and processes are shared by the different operational levels. It is important, therefore, that organisations pay sufficient attention to designing optimal overlap of 'roles and goals'. That is not to say that there is unnecessary duplication, rather, the organisation provides a 'multi-layered net' (Garvin and Levesque 2008) that is capable of dealing with systemic threats through shared accountability. Hence, service performance issues are shared at all operational levels rather than being 'outsourced' to front-line operatives. Best-practice companies have balanced scorecard mechanisms that translate into KPIs that are remarkably consistent from the top down, lending consistency of purpose and line of sight.

- *Gates and 'filtration' processes*: Prior to initiatives being launched, effective MUEs ensure releases are regulated and 'sense checked' prior to release. It is at this point – between conception and implementation – that best-practice MUEs deploy resources that focus upon shaping and moulding the content and process of initiatives into workable solutions. Initiatives that flow from the centre in an unfettered manner, without any input from personnel with direct operational experience, are likely to fail. In addition to this 'moulding' activity, well-designed multi-unit enterprises have structural checks and balances in place sifting the quality and quantity of information that flows from the centre to the units. In some organisations, specific support function roles are assigned at the centre, such as operational services managers (OSMs) who will oversee ERP systems (with a calendar of events and releases), regulating the flow of initiatives and new policies to the units. In ideal circumstances, OSMs work closely with decision makers in the line to decide whether or not specific information releases or initiatives are commensurate with operational priorities, preventing the onward transmission of non-value-added instructions. In some organisations, information releases and downloads are restricted to certain times of the day (usually pre-opening) or week (typically Friday) in order to prevent distracting unit managers with a constant barrage of data.

- *Feedback loops*: Another best-practice design principle is the use of feedback loops from the line to the centre which afford real-time information on 'hypertrends' and the impact and success of certain products/initiatives. For instance, at Zara (owned by Spanish firm Intedex) qualitative feedback is collected on the latest launches from unit managers by the centre the day after placement and, when linked to quantitative data, informs decision making on succeeding ranges. Many MUEs hold regular feedback sessions between operators and senior managers, considering a range of issues such as which product lines work, which practice changes are required and what operational improvements can be made to increase efficiency and effectiveness.

- *Re-set mechanisms*: One of the main problems that multi-unit organisations have is sets of legacy practices and systems that have lost their relevance. Organisations are notoriously bad at reviewing and reducing redundant reportage, 'red tape' and ossified operational instructions. However, some MUEs make regular efforts to 're-set' their operations following regular reviews of all their practices and procedures. They generally do this by taking a unit every couple of years and analysing all its systems, policies, practices and processes. In doing so, they ask the following questions: what is mandatory for legal and operational excellence and what is superfluous or 'nice to have'? Experimentation then follows, resetting operations in the pilot unit, measuring outcomes with regards to process and operational efficiency, and then making the interventions that worked/improved operations standard across the estate.

- *Rapid decision forums*: Another feature of best-practice design is the presence of decision-making forums with the authority to make instant or rapid decisions. Outside of the normal monthly central meeting cycle of product, HR, promotions, pricing and capital executives, some MUEs have lines of communications – for instance daily operational conference calls – where a select number of unit managers representing their area/region can seek instant solutions to practical operational problems. This process tends to work when it is chaired by a senior operational executive, lending it credibility and force. Also, participants in the process must have reached a level of insight and maturity which ensures that only issues of consequence are raised for a high-quality debate.

Case Study 2: Reshaping Architecture and Processes at UKCafé

The following is a case study written by Chris Conchie (MSc MUL, 2014) based upon his interview with the Head of Communications at UKCafé (pseudonym) as part of his research into how MUEs centrally control and co-ordinate plans/initiatives. UKCafé is a 'better' UK coffee chain with 500+ units in the UK and internationally.

... When we started to put our controls in place, the situation within UKCafé was a very different one. There was no real thought given to how new things were to be launched into the business, and what role meetings would play in the process... We had got ourselves into a position where things were launched poorly and/or failed soon after they began... Levels of execution were poor and our team and manager feedback sessions [indicated that] this was becoming the number one frustration... We took a step back from all of this, reviewed all of the planned activity and initiatives for the year ahead and, even with an initial quick review, we saw a bottleneck around September, as lots of activity 'piled up' for Xmas. ...

[So what did we do? First,] we split the activities into 10 equal parts and spread them across the year... this caused great initial pain as some activity had to be put back or even dropped from the calendar – painful for the heads of department (HODs) who had to change their plans to bring them in line... [Second] we started to hold monthly meetings with the HODs to allow them the opportunity to engage and help build the twelve-month activity plan – the agreement being that if their plans weren't passed through the communications team and factored into the plan, they wouldn't be rolled out to the business... [Third] we had to build in some degree of flexibility, some room for exceptions – if the price of milk increases unexpectedly we have to react quickly but these things can still be managed and we have agreed processes in place to deal with emergencies... [Fourth] every project was given a board sponsor to ensure that the business benefit was clear and supported by the senior leadership team... [Fifth] regional meetings are held every four weeks between the operations managers and the area managers... here area managers are

CONTINUED ...

given content through a set agenda for their meetings the following week… the commitment from the Communications Department being that this content will take up no more than one hour in briefing (this assumes a three-hour overall meeting); leaving time for area managers to concentrate on an area-specific agenda.

… Don't get me wrong, there is still a constant push back to stop anyone crashing these agendas but that is what my role is here for… feedback from the AMs/GMs has been excellent as they have felt more in control… Lots of our GMs are graduates or in their first management role; they need support on communication as this is not one of their key skills – meetings and paperwork are not what they are recruited for! …

Also, to get our feedback (in the absence of engagement surveys), we hold what we call 'cultural events' throughout the year… These consist of:

- *Barista Village*: hosted by Operations Director and HR Manager with one or two people invited per area; over 100 people every time. One of these is held per region per year. The staff members invited are asked their views and what they think of everything that affects them. This is our chance to get their feedback… everything they say is noted and the minutes are distributed to the relevant HOD.
- *Assistant Manager Days*: hosted by the Regional Manager and the CEO with 70–100 invited assistant managers from across the business. All forthcoming activity is discussed… The great benefit is that the CEO is able to ask questions of the assistants and they can ask him any questions… again all of the points are noted and fed back to the business…
- *Emerging Manager Days*: are twice a year held for up and coming managers who are highlighted for development – these sessions involve visits to HO and lunch with the board…
- *Club Champions*: essentially our way of recognising long-serving staff… these twice a year sessions are very informal chats and dinners but they are a great opportunity for the staff to get involved and for the board to meet and get feedback from key people within the workforce…

Indeed, effective architecture and process design is an important aspect of MUE differential advantage, namely the degree to which firms have superior operational capabilities which transform inputs through a number of value-added process stages into valuable outputs (Slack et al. 2009). 'Transforming inputs' – staff, technology, buildings and machines – underpin the vital processes that service 'transformed inputs' such as customers, materials and information. These 'transforming inputs' – such as the operational team, IT systems (incorporating ERP planning systems, EPOS customer order capture, replenishment systems etc.), warehousing, fleet and logistics, and so forth – are vital components of MUE firm success. If these capabilities can be leveraged over multiple formats/brands in any given territory, then firms are able to extend their 'efficient frontiers of production' through effective asset optimisation.

THREE KEY 'ARCHITECTURE AND PROCESS' QUESTIONS FOR MUE DECISION MAKERS

1. Do you have effective channels in place to cascade information, plans, initiatives and changes (downwards and upwards)?
2. Do you have *empowered* 'air traffic controllers' in place to 'sense check', regulate and 'filter' the flow of information from the centre to the line?
3. Do you regularly review your policies asking yourself what you should 'stop, start or continue' mandating?

SUMMARY

This chapter attempts to bring some organisational context to the AM role by elucidating some of the challenges faced by contemporary MUEs and giving a truncated account of their responses. But what does the above analysis tell us about how MUEs try and mitigate the effects of distance from an organisational perspective? In effect, many of the 'macro' challenges posed to MUEs – particularly those which have taken an international path – are related to issues such as *institutional*, *power* and *cultural* (*psychic*) distance (see Edger 2013). The degree to which international MUE parent companies (IMUEs) can close down these forms of distance by custom-ising their products and policies has a major influence upon whether or not they are successful. For instance IMUEs with a high level of service in their product mix will find that – due to prevailing institutional and cultural idiosyncrasies in developing markets – they will have to work to 'see the differences' and nuances in order to adapt their service concepts accordingly (Edger 2013). The experiential and perceptual skills of policy makers are therefore extremely important in 'melding the offer' to eliminate dissonance and detachment.

At a 'micro' organisational level, the challenges faced by MUEs also triangulate with the multiple dimensions of distance (see 'Distance Literature' in Chapter 1). *Structurally*, the enforcement of product consistency is hampered by spatial distance – as indeed, is the act of local market customisation. *Functionally*, centre-versus-local tensions exemplify 'outsider'-versus-'insider' tensions highlighted by many scholars commentating within the leader–member distance domain (Bligh and Riggio 2013). *Psychologically*, format proliferation poses problems to organisations in terms of engagement (through 'two-speed' estates) and appropriate person–job fit.

This inevitably begs the question as to what the dominant organisational responses are to these issues of distance. Recasting the analysis presented in 'Organisational Responses' above, from a *psychological* perspective, clear strategic positioning, strong leadership and a positive cultural environment (with high levels of engagement-led HRM) increase the proximity of senior policy makers to followers in MUEs. By the same token, architectural design can be viewed as a *structural* response to decrease hierarchical/physical distance hampering implementation/ consistency whilst simultaneously reducing *functional* 'outsider'-versus-'insider' tensions. Continuing these themes, the degree to which the AM role is designed will – in theory – also reduce the multiple dimensions of distance hampering MUE performance, something which is addressed in the following chapter.

CHAPTER 3
OPERATIONAL EXCELLENCE

Having considered the environmental and organisational context/challenges of the multi-unit enterprise (MUE), it is now appropriate to consider what activities organisations expect area managers (AMs) to undertake to reduce the *distance* between policy-maker intention and practical execution. This chapter will examine the functions of the AM by, *first*, looking at their prime activities – usually denominated as 'operational excellence' – in the order that organisations generally prioritise them, namely: implementing operational systems, ensuring standards adherence and sales-led service execution. *Second*, the manner in which they address these activities will be discussed with particular reference to the way they are measured and are mandated to plan their time. *Third*, the chapter will consider the particular issues and problems that AMs feel they have in discharging their functions, using empirical evidence to highlight dominant themes and issues. The argument that will be followed in this chapter is that most multi-unit enterprises examined during the course of my research, due to the aforementioned disruptive forces and micro-challenges of the multi-unit firm, have placed inordinate emphasis on operational systems compliance at the expense of service execution. The net effect upon AMs is that they feel that they are merely transmission mechanisms for enforcement and punishment, a state which elicits stress, anxiety and paralysis. The following chapters ('Commitment', 'Control', 'Change' and 'Characteristics and Development') will outline the professional practice that effective AMs exercise to overcome these challenges and the personal characteristics they need in order to do so.

SYSTEMS IMPLEMENTATION

In order to assist the operational line, the blueprint of most retail and leisure brands systematically details all the operating functions which must be performed at unit level including their particular characteristics, responsibilities and timings. Often, enterprises will have multiple blueprints for different operational processes, standards and sales-led service duties that might be conducted independently or simultaneously. Imperatives detailed within job descriptions, procedural manuals, KPIs, balanced scorecards or incentive schemes are usually an attempt to leverage those elements of the operational blueprint (i.e. systems, standards and service) that the organisation deems critical to its success.

However, the starting point for operational excellence is the proper application of an MUE's systems and associated processes. Many of these might be invisible to the customer (invariably being situated 'back of house') but they have an enormous impact upon the standards and service levels that customer's experience. The operational system can be defined as a series of interlocking, critically dependent processes which are concerned with turning materials, information and/or customers into value-added outputs through the intervention of 'transforming inputs' such as staff, technology and buildings (Slack et al. 2009). To a large extent, process success is contingent on the correct strategy and design principles being followed by the multi-unit enterprise prior to implementation, with review mechanisms ensuring correction and improvement. Strategy, design and review apart, however, the main objective of AMs is to ensure that the vital processes flow efficiently, meeting prime objectives of cost, speed, quality, dependability and flexibility. Whilst it is impossible to detail, within the confines of this book, the diversity of multi-unit enterprise operational systems and processes, it is important to highlight the key processes that our research found organisations deemed critical elements of the AM role at this time.

The first area for which AMs are responsible, indeed the starting point for understanding the role, comprises all processes that relate to cost control and procedural/legal compliance. The degree to which organisations place an overdue emphasis on these areas will be dealt with later on in this chapter; but there is little doubt that – whatever the rhetoric that many organisations wrap around the role – a main qualifier for AM is to 'get the substance of the role right'. The dominant systems and processes which AMs are expected to oversee in most MUEs are as follows:

a) *Labour Processes*

- Labour ratio tracking: Ensure units keep to forecast and/or budget/cash target

- Rostering and deployment: Ensure that units are fully manned to undertake duties required during peak and non-peak trading sessions; check seasonal rostering plans and ensure sufficient labour capacity to service volume; check 'right person, right place, right time'; check for 'ghosting' (i.e. staff that are on the payroll but are not working at the establishment)

- Employment law compliance: Ensure that units are operating legally and in accordance to cultural/religious norms (e.g. following working time rules, migrant diaspora workers have permits/passports, proper age, gender and diversity regulatory/religious adherence etc.)

- Unions: Deal with local representatives of organised labour where necessary; ensure good relations are sustained for operational efficiency purposes

b) *Standard Operating Procedures*

- Back-of-house (BOH) tasks: Ensure standard back-of-house task lists and section 'details' are adhered to (e.g. data uploads, delivery checks, storage, security etc.); monitor food production procedural adherence within catering and dining contexts

- Front-of-house (FOH) tasks: Monitor front-of-house tasks such as: pre-opening procedural adherence, 'daily duty manager' sweeps, section accounting, till procedures etc.

c) *Availability, Stock and Waste Processes*

- Availability: Ensure appropriate stockholding is in place to service demand; monitor replenishment and check supply chain to ensure constant availability

- Reconciliation: Ensure cash takings reconcile with sales and stock

- Theft and shrinkage: Check security and surveillance processes to minimise pilfering, 'knock-offs' and shrinkage

- Waste: Monitor and minimise non-consumable *and* perishable waste

d) *Sales and Pricing Monitoring*

- Daily/Weekly sales: Check daily and weekly sales against budget and last year
- Timeslot analysis: Monitor sales flows by timeslot; check throughputs and efficiency
- Pricing accuracy: Check coding exception reports; ensure pricing accuracy
- Ad hoc discounting: Check 'end of line'/'out of date' pricing and sales times (too early?)

e) *Due Diligence and Essential Maintenance Processes*

- Safety: Check fire safety compliance (testing, extinguishers etc.); monitor on-site customer incident book
- Hygiene: Check adherence to statutory and company procedures; ensure food hygiene standards are compliant (e.g. 100% food hygiene training for food handlers); check pest and rodent control systems; all equipment maintained and serviced?
- Legal compliance: 100% under-age alcohol sales training (in territories where legally permitted)
- Hazards: Ensure all essential maintenance requests are actioned on time and to specification

f) *Ad Hoc Processes/Change Initiatives*

- Pre-opening: Oversee new opening processes: staffing, stocking, training, handover etc.
- Local suppliers: Maintain and monitor 'local suppliers' list (product and maintenance contractors)
- New product launches: Train for and communicate new product launches
- Change initiatives: Act as conduit for all new change initiatives (e.g. promotions, operations systems etc.)
- New site locations: Scan for new site opportunities

STANDARDS ADHERENCE

In addition to monitoring and implementing back-of-house systems and processes for cost and compliance purposes, MULs have a large role to play in enforcing front-of-house standards, ensuring the customer-facing store environment is kept to a high standard:

a) *Merchandising and Display*

- Planogram checks: Ensure merchandise is displayed according to specification (e.g. facings and perishable range display)
- Promotions: Check promotions (signage, posters, shelf pricing, gondola ends etc.)

b) *Internal Environmental Management*

- Cleanliness: Check cleaning rota and cleanliness (especially toilets and trading areas); in addition, check BOH stock rooms, staff changing and rest rooms etc. – the cleanliness of these areas will be linked to FOH standards
- Sound, lighting and 'smell': Ensure all 'sensory' sound, lighting and (where appropriate) 'smell' systems are functioning appropriately; check speaker systems and background music loops; ensure the store is properly lit for security, safety and product illumination purposes; check 'perfume' and ersatz 'odour' systems
- Air conditioning and heating: Check functionality and effectiveness
- Fixtures and fittings: Ensure fixtures and fitting are maintained and presented to the required standard
- Store security: Check the robustness of the store security systems (both mechanical and human)

c) *External Environment*

- External agencies: Fulfil a troubleshooting, problem resolution and *'relationship'* role with local officials, authorities, land-lords, environmental health, safety executives and external auditing agencies engaged by the organisation
- Competitive scanning: Monitor local competitive activity; respond (where permitted) and/or feedback to senior management/head office (if feedback loops in place)
- Social responsibility: Check links with local community (e.g. charities, fund raising, job schemes, perishable food distribution etc.)
- Local PR: Ensure units have a high degree of local visibility through the local press

SALES-LED SERVICE EXECUTION

Clearly systems/process efficiency and standards adherence are important inputs into service effectiveness. In addition, as the previous chapter outlined, the business model of the multi-unit enterprise influences the elements of service that are an operational necessity in order to guarantee customer satisfaction. Organisations operating in a low-cost paradigm are more likely to concentrate upon functional speed and efficiency whilst firms seeking differentiation will emphasise emotional attributes of service: staff politeness, knowledge and engagement. Customers will have pre-set service expectations based on variables such as price as to the levels of service that they will receive; service companies must ensure at the very least that they ensure that their perceptions (i.e. judgement as to *actual* levels of service) meet these expectations (Johnston and Clarke 2008). Managing the perception–expectation gap is a science that many multi-unit enterprises are devoting a lot of time and resources to at present, the execution of which is a key function of the AM.

In order to impact levels of sales-led service execution, AMs are generally tasked with the following functions:

a) ***Unit-based HR***
- Roles and responsibilities: Check that roles and responsibilities are clearly denominated, assigned and understood; in particular, ensure shift leaders have clearly specified pre- and in-session duties and tasks
- Recruitment and selection: Appoint managers and assistants with appropriate behaviours and capabilities; check store recruitment systems and hiring mechanisms to ensure 'meritocratic' attitudinal and skills testing
- Coaching and training: Ensure that appropriate coaching and training mechanisms (in terms of operational requirements AND culture/language) are in place and are being rigorously followed
- Compensation: Check compensation levels against local market; ensure that sufficient talent is being attracted and retained; check behavioural effectiveness of PRP targets and fairness/efficacy of the tipping system/tronque (where it exists)

- Performance appraisal: Ensure that regular team/staff appraisals are taking place to the required standards of development and performance metrics
- Store leadership: Check and audit staff satisfaction/engagement, absence, grievance data etc.

b) *Service Concept Adherence*
  - Service flow: Ensure that customer 'touches' are applied in the appropriate manner (sympathetic to local cultural norms) at each stage of the service cycle

c) *Customer Survey Follow-up*
  - Mystery customer: Monitor and action outputs from mystery-customer visits
  - Online surveys: Monitor and action outputs from online survey data
  - Web-based feedback: Regularly check and (where permitted) answer feedback on web-based forums and channels

d) *Service Promise and Complaints Resolution*
  - Service promise: Check that the service promise (e.g. no quibble return) is fulfilled – particularly in relation to 'click and collect' services
  - Complaints: Ensure that complaints are answered and rectified both in-store and at head office in accordance with company procedure

REPORTS AND MEASUREMENT

The practices which AMs actually deploy to expedite the dimensions of operational excellence cited above will be dealt with in the succeeding three chapters ('Commitment', 'Control' and 'Change'); but how do MUEs generally report upon and/or measure the activities cited above? The answer is that data for measuring 'operational excellence' is generally bundled into daily, weekly and monthly reports. AMs can access data through web intelligence reports and, increasingly, through vehicles such as daily reporting apps (which generally convey sales and labour data). As will be discussed later, the main issue for AMs (particularly those new to the role or organisation) is the volume, frequency, accuracy and format in which the data is conveyed and the fairness/equity of their KPIs and incentives.

- **KPIs and incentives**: Typically, AMs have KPIs which are clustered around three main areas: business/operations, customers and employees. Generic metrics include:
  - **Business/operational KPIs**: Sales (revenue and/or items), margin, labour, other management costs (non-consumables, energy, waste, shrinkage etc.), safety, availability etc.
  - **Customer KPIs**: Mystery-customer scores (net promoter, overall satisfaction, individual elements such as knowledge, speed and quality) and complaints (per cheque or transaction)
  - **Employee KPIs**: Satisfaction, turnover, stability and succession.

Different sectors within the multi-unit universe are apt to apply disproportionate incentive weightings to metrics that are regarded specific drivers of commercial success: retail supermarkets (availability), leisure (new member recruitment), builders' merchants (active accounts), retail banks (new accounts and cross-sales), fast food (speed of service), casual dining (food quality), hotels (revenue per average room) and apparel (stock movement).

Incentives are generally structured for annual performance with some element of tactical quarterly bonuses (usually relating to labour targets). Overall, the multi-unit enterprises examined for this research tended to concentrate more on business and operational metrics (e.g. outcomes) rather than employee and customer metrics.

- **Formal appraisals**: Formal performance measurement against these KPIs was generally assessed and monitored through performance and competency-based appraisal systems:
  - **Performance appraisals**: These usually include 'balanced scorecard' KPIs outlined above. As stated, the weightings that organisations applied to each measure varied relative to sector, but also culture, business model and/or competitive position.
  - **Competency assessment**: Often organisations had input competency measurements for AMs, against which they are scored according to range statement 'fit'. One organisation had six competencies: 'leading to win, understanding organisations, interpreting people, curiosity, impact and influencing, and courage and conviction'. Issues with using such methodology relate to its validity, interpretation and 'real life' application.

- **League tables**: League tables were regularly used method of performance measurement in multi-unit enterprises. They helped organisations to calibrate general performance against the mean whilst generating competition amongst AMs within specific regions or areas. Common league tables included: stock control, training compliance, hygiene scores, margin, wastage, labour turnover and/or staff stability, customer service, voids and refunds etc. The degree to which these tables were genuinely used as a 'carrot' or another form of subtle 'stick' with which to beat AMs is a moot point. Many respondents in the research for this book had a view which accorded with the latter – that in many cases league tables were there to name and shame rather than recognise and praise.

PLANNING AND ORGANISING

In order to ensure that AMs discharged their responsibilities effectively, most MUEs offered guidance (sometimes mandatory) on how they *should* allocate their time to maximum effect. In extreme circumstances, companies dictated the minutiae of AM movement: for instance, one organisation used a vehicle-based telematics tracking system that recorded AM journeys to ensure that they kept to their defined 'structured ways of working' parameters! The following schedule is an example of how one organisation mandates its AMs (who have 15 sites each) to use their time:

Activity	Days	
Admin, Planning and Action	47	(1 day per week)
Unit Strategy Meetings	30	(2 days a year per location)
Unit Operating Reviews	30	(2 days a year per location)
District Meetings	9	
Unit Mgr. Appraisals	10	(2 x 5 days one location)
Flexible Days	74	(1.5 days per week)
Area Meetings	12	
Conferences/Roadshows	4	
Quarterly Appraisal	4	
Profit Review	6	(0.5 days per month)
Total	*226*	

(Time Available: 260 working days minus 34 days holiday = 226 days)

Figure 3.1 AM Activity Planner

In terms of the major activities, AMs are expected to use their time in a specific manner:

- **Administration, action and planning days**: AMs typically spend a day working from home, examining their reporting pages (sales, cash, costs and stock) and web intelligence (hygiene and margins) in order to analyse the performance of their units and decide on any remedial action required. It is also an opportunity to examine e-mails relating to new initiatives and promotions and consider actions that might be pending relating to forthcoming promotions, initiatives, capital investment etc. In organisations with central planning systems, AMs can review and consider the calendar of activities scheduled for the next month. It is also an opportunity for AMs to phone and e-mail their units to chase up specific issues and, in some cases, take the opportunity of having telephone conference calls which involve the whole district in order to monitor and review the progress of particular priorities. Although some companies have tried to introduce e-mail embargos for AMs and their units during the week, with specific downloads only allowed at pre-set times of the week, it is common, with current technology, for AMs to devote another 15 hours per week at various other times to administration and progress chasing by phone and/or e-mail.

- **Business strategy meetings**: This meeting is intended to be a forward-looking meeting in which past performance is reviewed through analysis of the balanced scorecard (people, customers, sales and profit) as a basis for future action. The AM meets the unit manager on-site to observe the business and the offer delivery in order to agree specified actions which should be recorded on an agreed action plan. This meeting is designed to be different from performance appraisals or compliance reviews as it concentrates on the actions that will improve the execution of the offer through people deployment and, where allowable, targeted promotions.

- **Operating review meetings**: This meeting – sometimes called the standards or due diligence review – is designed to concentrate solely on operational compliance aspects of the business. In essence these visits are about keeping the site 'safe and legal' through ensuring that the business is fully compliant with legal and company regulations (by checking the bookwork, interviewing the manager and staff, and personal observation).

Thus, in casual dining environments, the AM will conduct a staff-and-guest safety review examining areas such as the kitchen, checking hygiene and safety standard compliance. The unit's due-diligence paperwork will be reviewed to ensure that operatives are monitoring fridge and food preparation temperatures, undertaking mandatory training programmes for new starters and carrying out vital health and safety precautions such as regular pest control visits. In multiple retail environments, the AM will check items such as the customer incident book, security systems, trading standards documentation (such as under-18 alcoholic drink sales refusals) and hazard maintenance progress. In all sectors, the AM will be expected to check the front-of-house standards of the operation, very often with a pre-designed checklist that produces an overall 'compliance score' for the business.

ISSUES

There are a number of issues that relate to the way the role is structured and the key functions that are expected to be fulfilled. In the main, most AMs surveyed for this book believed that due to the role's emphasis on controls, there is little time to address value-added commitment-based activities. The principal issues highlighted were undue emphasis on compliance (which undermined their authority and capacity for action), the pressure they felt they were under to punish rather than reward, and their immense workload. These will be considered in turn.

- *Compliance focus*: The major issue with standard multi-unit enterprises is the degree to which complying with the myriad of controls and procedures becomes an end in itself rather than an enabler for running truly great businesses. In many cases, organisations placed far more emphasis on 'doing it right' rather than 'doing the right things'. Issues such as service and improving the offer are put on the back burner as AMs and their unit managers are compelled to concentrate on compliance minutiae to the detriment of improving the product. One major survey in a major MUE found that AMs believed that they spent over 50% of their time, whilst onsite, on 'compliance and checking' activities; with as little as 8% of their time devoted to coaching and training and 12% on reviewing performance. Other aspects of compliance which AMs are expected to enact, amplified by the recent economic downturn, have included monitoring and limiting labour ratios, maintenance spend, wastage and stock losses. In the case of labour ratios, some firms abandoned their extant systems imposing strict daily and/or weekly labour cash targets that units were not permitted to exceed.

- **Enforcement and punishment**: A natural consequence of having compliance regimes is that they must be enforced. My earlier research discovered that many AMs spent a lot of time 'chasing compliance' and, in many cases, felt under inordinate pressure from the centre to apply sanctions for non-conformance. For some acts of non-compliance, many multi-unit enterprises provided strict disciplinary guidelines for AMs to apply for issues such as stock losses or hygiene breaches. Whatever the extenuating circumstances (e.g. lack of labour, resources or unrealistic stretch targets) AMs were expected to enforce strict disciplinary sanctions to non-conformance/breaches of BRAG (black, red, amber, green) reports.

- **Overload and inaccuracy**: Given the spans of control that AMs have in most MUEs and the time they spend travelling between units (up to 30% in some organisations), it is essential that organisations are judicious in the allocation of tasks and data analysis expected of this operational cohort. It is clear that the amount of blueprint standards and procedures that AMs are expected to regulate is significant but, when coupled with overlays, changes and amendments, the workload for most MULs is vast. Most AMs interviewed agreed that it was almost impossible to analyse, cover and/or enforce every single policy, procedure or measure produced by the organisation. In one company, a study showed that each unit was subject to over 400 measures per week, meaning that the AM was, theoretically, confronted by nearly 23,000 metrics per month to check their district against. Factoring in the fact that data is frequently inaccurate or misleading, it is very difficult for AMs to prioritise or convert data into meaningful information. A complicating factor might lie in the fact that many reports come from different sources within the organisation and, as previously stated, are presented on different systems and in different formats due to legacy IT infrastructure. The AM is expected to interpret and prioritise this data into actionable outcomes, often with little assistance from the centre. Also, organisational priorities might change, thereby complicating the work of the AM. A suite of reports that the

AM has relied upon as key performance metrics might become redundant if the organisation places emphasis on a new set of priorities.

As a result there are a number of outcomes relating to these issues cited above that bedevil the role, many of which have serious operational consequences:

- **'Busy fools'**: AMs experiencing the above issues were apt to refer to themselves as 'firefighters'. One cohort of AMs surveyed for Edger (2012) believed that, in addition to the 50% of their time spent on compliance monitoring, a further 20% was spent creating 'patch ups' and 'workarounds' to unworkable policies and initiatives.

- **Fear and loathing**: A natural consequence of the imposition of a compliance culture was that AMs developed a fear of 'the faceless bureaucrats at head office'. The notion that somebody was monitoring them over such a vast range of metrics, some of which were bound to be in negative territory at various junctures, fuelled feelings of resentment, anxiety and loathing.

- **Stress and paralysis**: It is of little surprise that such feelings commonly led to high levels of stress within this cohort. In one organisation with an excessively control-type regime, compounded by the economic crisis, 12% of AMs were signed off sick with 'stress-related illnesses' at one particular point. Those that were left were faced with increased workloads. Thus, discretionary effort drops, innovation and creativity is stifled and AMs survive and 'satisfice' rather than optimise the business.

- **Infantilisation**: Another outcome of compliance, enforcement and overload was the degree to which AMs felt, in the words of one, that being 'treated like children made us act like children'. Thus, in an extreme reaction to their perceived environment, reasonable requests from head office were now subject to routine cynicism, with some AMs 'complaining and moaning just for the sake of it'. Mature AMs, worn down by the constant demands and strictures issued from the centre, started to behave badly.

- **Going native**: The degree to which AMs identify more with the needs of their units than the organisation is another issue created in extreme compliance cultures. There are two explanations for this. First, some AMs side with their units because of what they perceive as the injustices of the unreasonable demands and metrics they believe are being meted out; in this respect, AMs see themselves as the guardians of their people and districts. Second, there are those AMs that will side with their unit managers for self-interested purposes. Given their own performance needs, AMs recognise that in order to maintain some semblance of order and discipline they need to demonstrate, both in word and deed, their support for their people. The problem with going native, however, is that it can potentially undermine the ability of the organisation to make merited changes and drive strategy. To what extent are AMs good judges of what is actually beneficial or detrimental for their units? There comes a point, as one operations director put it, at which some AMs 'have completely lost their marbles and fight anything that is introduced on the basis that if it has come from the centre, it must be bad!'

- *Resistance and sabotage*: Such feelings of fear and stress often manifested themselves in other ways such as through acts of wilful non-conformance. Evidence of resistance was common, with AMs recounting their ways of getting around 'the system' with relish. In terms of low-level resistance, some AMs admitted refusing to acknowledge e-mails or return phone calls, ignoring requests for information or central dictates on purpose. At the extreme end, there is evidence that some AMs engaged in deliberate sabotage through slowing processes down or issuing incorrect instructions.

The unintended consequences of operating an unrelenting compliance culture are the very antithesis of what the organisation was seeking to achieve in the first place! This research found that the outcomes were actually opposite to those intended, resulting in less control and worse performance:

- *Less control*: The outcome of operating an unrelenting compliance culture – where enforcement and overload rules – is that the organisation has less rather than more control. Accountabilities are avoided for fear of retribution, discretionary effort collapses and key people leave, draining the organisation of vital knowledge capital.

- *Worse performance*: As an accompaniment to deteriorating control and alignment, performance suffers. Put simply, organisations that were doing well do less well and those doing badly perform worse.

SUMMARY

The introduction and context chapter hinted at the reasons why so many multi-unit enterprises lean towards a compliance-type mentality, including the need for the centre to apply strict controls in order to ensure standardisation and consistency within the *dispersed* geographical form of the multi-unit enterprise. But in trying to *'reduce' distance* with the units through a myriad of control procedures, MUEs often achieve the opposite by 'pushing them away' through excessive compliance regimes. Metric/initiative overload increases the *physical distance* between the AM and their units, limiting the frequency of social/emotional interaction and accentuating *hierarchical distance* between the centre and the field. Excessive levels of *functional distance* open up where operational 'ingroups' engage in infantilised behaviour against support function 'outgroups'. Exclusive concentration on compliance (whatever its accompanying rhetoric) also accentuates aspects of *cultural/demographic distance* between the AM and their followers/customers because – being wrapped up in compliance minutiae – they do not have enough time/capacity to understand their needs, desires and motivations. AMs become *detached* from the *vocational* imperatives of their roles because of the one-dimensional approach they are being forced to adopt.

Thus, the consequences of applying a compliance approach to the exclusion of everything else can have serious ramifications in terms of *increasing* rather than *decreasing structural, psychological and functional distance*, posing serious threats to the long-term financial performance of the firm, squeezing entrepreneurialism, innovation and discretionary effort. How do AMs assert some semblance of authority, legitimacy and consent in order to operate effectively in such in an environment? How do they *'close down' distance* with both their units and the centre? The following three chapters will explore how effective AMs address this conundrum, applying commitment, control and change-based practices that enable them *to lead at a distance with MUEs*.

COMMITMENT

In the work of behavioural social scientists, commitment is portrayed as a construct which determines an individual's psychological attachment to her or his firm. The higher the levels of an individual's positive emotional attachment to an organisation, the more likely they are to 'commit' to the firm's goals/objectives and exert discretionary effort. But is organisational commitment necessarily the main determinant of positive attachment, given the *distance* of the centre from the units within multi-unit enterprises (MUEs)? The previous chapter has outlined a number of barriers that confront area managers (AMs) in attempting to discharge the main functions of their role (e.g. pursuance of operational excellence through systems implementation, standards adherence and sales-led service execution), potentially eroding their own personal, and their teams', commitment to the organisation. Yet my earlier research uncovered effective AMs who outperformed their peers in both benign and adverse organisational contexts – so how do effective AMs generate commitment within their own sphere of influence to ensure that they achieve operational excellence? What specific *local leadership practices* do they deploy to achieve this? First, this chapter will consider the meaning of commitment from an academic standpoint and its importance for AMs within MUEs. Second, the *local leadership practices* which AMs exercise to elicit commitment amongst their teams and direct reports will be considered, including a *vision and clear direction*, creation of a *sales-led service culture*, *talent attraction and development*, *team working* and *trust and recognition*.

UNDERSTANDING COMMITMENT

ACADEMIC COMMENTARY

The term commitment, used liberally by practitioners and organisational commentators alike, is usually intended to denote worker willingness, readiness or positive mindset. To this extent, it takes an attitudinal perspective, its principal meaning being related to ensuring that 'people's hearts and minds are in the right place'. The natural inference of the commitment hypothesis is that, if such a state of emotional attachment between workers and organisations is achieved, there will be a concomitant behavioural dividend, translating into performance outputs (Guest 1997). Some academics would argue that a better explanation for increased worker discretionary effort might be framed more effectively from other constructs such as 'engagement' or 'job satisfaction'. However, it can be argued that commitment provides a valid lens through which to understand effective area management, given that many of the practices that are designed to elicit commitment are connected to engagement and job satisfaction initiatives. In short, rather than accepting the position of some academics that there are differences between commitment, engagement and job satisfaction, the view of this author is that the three are intertwined and inextricably linked to one another.

It should be understood that in addition to commitment being understood as 'affective emotional mindset attachment' to the organisation, it can also be framed in terms of 'continuance' and 'normative' mindset attachments (Meyer and Allen 1991). Unlike the former 'affective' state, where the individual identifies willingly with the organisational goals, both 'continuance' and 'normative' perspectives conceive commitment as being applicable when individuals feel that they might either suffer cost as a result of not committing or feel an obligation to commit. 'Affective commitment' – deemed the most desirable mindset due to its voluntarism – is conceived as being most usually the output of *engagement interventions* such as: selecting the right people with the right values and attitude in the first place, putting in place a clear vision, mission and objectives, extensive two-way communications, teamwork and high investment in employee development. Hence inputs into commitment are conceived very much within the *service operations*, *leadership* and *HRM paradigms*, areas of enquiry that are extensively covered in Edger (2012, 2013).

AMS AND COMMITMENT

As has been outlined previously, the challenges facing AMs in multi-unit enterprises are significant. Situated between the centre and the units, AMs are expected to lead their units to deliver high levels of systems and process efficiency, superior standards and excellent sales-led service. This is in spite of the fact that, as outlined in the previous chapter, they are sometimes supplied with inaccurate data, faced with irreconcilable aims and demands and, in many organisations, an expectation that they are principally charged with control and compliance activities. The question remains as to how AMs are able to generate commitment in such hostile and ambiguous circumstances. What my earlier research found was that, in *both* benign and extreme contexts, effective AMs did similar things in order to generate commitment, although admittedly it was easier for AMs to achieve this in the former context. Thus, it can be argued that many of the instruments designed to elicit commitment can be denominated as being fairly universal, given their identification and observation in a range of situations.

Our start point for elucidating the commitment-based practices that AMs deploy to produce favourable outcomes is the fact that effective AMs concentrate on optimising their portfolio as a whole, rather than concentrating exclusively on managing individual units. To this extent, they should be seen as portfolio optimisers, utilising and deploying human capital and knowledge in the most effective manner across their districts. There are three reasons for this phenomenon:

- *Measurement*: AMs are measured and incentivised according to a district P&L and therefore their behaviour is likely to consider the performance of the whole rather than just the sum of its parts.
- *Resource optimisation*: Effective AMs recognise that in order to achieve optimal efficiency they have to utilise talent, knowledge and resource across the portfolio, particularly the areas of starvation that have huge growth potential if the right skills and knowledge are 'matched' effectively.
- *Distance*: Because of peer-group 'talent hoarding' and geographical distance, gaining access to resources outside the district is difficult. Effective AMs are therefore forced to arrange their own portfolio effectively rather than relying on outside help.

With regards to commitment, one particular quantitative experiment merits citation, carried out in 2009 in a market-leading MUE (44,000 employees in nearly 2,000 units). Here, unit-manager engagement data from 16 high-performing (HIPO) AMs was matched with that of 119 of their peers. These 16 AMs had been selected by the company as exemplars to be used in the construction of a new cross-company leadership framework. They had been selected on the basis of their demonstrated operational excellence – their prior three-year profit and sales performance, compliance record (health and safety, cash and stock and standards), employee engagement (stability and turnover) and customer satisfaction (speed of service, quality and politeness). Would these high-performing AMs demonstrate better unit-manager engagement scores than their peers and, if so, in what areas? What leadership characteristics did they demonstrate?

Following statistical analysis, the HIPO AMs were found to have significantly better engagement scores than their peers (i.e. *mean versus mean*) with better mean scores in relation to support and development, involvement, direction, resource allocation, camaraderie, and openness and honesty:

Engagement Question	Variance*
My manager and I regularly discuss how I could improve through training, coaching or development	+7.2%
My manager involves me in setting our team's goals	+6.9%
The manager of our team gives us clear guidance	+6.6%
I feel as though I get fair recognition for a job well done	+6.7%
I have the resources I need to do my job to the best of my ability	+5.4%
There is a good spirit in our team	+5.3%
My manager is open, respectful and honest with me	+4.2%
(*% deviation from mean versus mean)	

Table 4.1: HIPO AM Engagement Scores versus Peers

Two other findings emerged from this comparative analysis:

- **Reward**: HIPO AMs, while scoring disproportionately well in relation to their peers in 'personal supervisor support' attributes, rated slightly worse (-0.04%) in relation to the battery of questions relating to reward. This should be of little surprise as pay, conditions, budgets and incentives were set by the centre in this organisation – HIPO AMs had little control over this hygiene factor. It is significant, however, that their perception regarding reward did not contaminate their overall assessment of engagement factors relating to their AM.

- **Company strategy**: HIPO AM respondents scored the question 'I know what the company is working to achieve' -0.2% worse, which may suggest that they rated the local direction of their HIPO AM more highly than their understanding of a 'distant' company strategy.

Overall, this survey indicated that high-performing MULs achieved their results through effective local leadership practices, leveraging the human capital of their portfolio more effectively than their peers. But what are the commitment-based *practices* of effective MULs?

LOCAL VISION AND CLEAR DIRECTION

One of the universal leadership attributes preferred by followers, across all cultures, is a strong sense of direction supported by definitive values (House et al. 2004). All MUEs and, for the most part, their subsidiaries and affiliates, will have a binding long-term vision/view (with a three- to five-year horizon most typically) which elucidates a desired future state, a description of *where* the organisation wants to be. This is commonly connected to a mission statement which describes *what* the organisation does, supported by strategy/tactics which say *how* they are going to achieve their aims (often incorporated into a balanced scorecard), underpinned by a value set that outlines the behaviours that members of the firm need to display in order to make it happen. These superordinate statements, usually crafted by senior policy makers, are cascaded throughout the organisation by a variety of means. They typically form the backbone of internal corporate communication, with core messages from these statements being reinforced at every opportunity through CEO communications, briefings, town-hall meetings and so forth.

The issue that AMs have at a local level is that sometimes these high-level statements of intent seem, at best, *abstract* and *detached*, at worst, irrelevant (see survey results on 'Company Strategy' above). Views relating to the organisation within the portfolio will be dependent upon where sites are within the investment cycle and what support and resources members are receiving from the organisation to expedite the stated objectives. At times, members might feel that such superordinate statements and goals are rhetoric, warm words that are unsupported by reality. For instance, an MUE might say that *what* it exists to do is to 'become the leading *x* through constantly delighting its customers', supported by grand pronouncements as to *how* it will achieve this through 'passionate and motivated colleagues', underpinned by values of 'tolerance, respect and integrity' but then act in a totally inconsistent, contrary manner by reducing staffing and maintenance spend to a minimum when it begins to struggle. The way in which effective AMs deal with this ambiguity is to create a sense of purpose and mission pertinent to their particular contexts. AMs need to create a binding commitment to what they are trying to achieve amongst their followers within their portfolios, in order to guide collective effort and energy. As the AM is measured at a portfolio level, (s)he must find a means by which every member of her/his team can articulate *what* they (as a team) are trying to do and *how* they are going to do it. But *how* do AMs construct a local vision that drives self-regulating, collective behaviours *and* a high degree of followership? Also, which forums should AMs utilise to drive consensual behaviours and maintain a clear direction?

HOW TO CREATE A LOCAL VISION

- **Share**: Distribute information on company/brand vision, strategy and objectives
- **Involve**: Lead team in an open discussion on aspects that are of particular local relevance or have a high resonance:
  - understand company/brand objectives (weighting and importance)
  - calibrate district gaps against higher objectives/priorities (i.e. operational, customer, colleague and community)
  - agree input and output linkages/dependencies
  - set aspirational goals/targets to close the gap; define what success looks like
  - agree measurement, 'improvement monitors', responsibilities and feedback mechanisms
  - cascade to the wider team with a 'local vision' (that addresses the 'why') and set of objectives/tactics which engender:
    - recall – abbreviations or patterns of numbers that are memorable

- realism – stretching but realistic superordinate district goals, creating a sense of optimistic momentum
- **Recognition**: Ensure there are sufficient reward and recognition devices in place to motivate and engage team members

Case Study 3: Local Vision and Clear Direction in Gibbs & Dandy

Tony Taylor is one of two operations directors for Gibbs & Dandy (16 units), a fast-growing chain of specialist builders' merchants owned by St Gobain (owners of the Jewson and Grahams chains – circa 800 units – in the UK).

… At Gibbs & Dandy we operate a portfolio of specialist builders' merchants that concentrate on fulfilling local market needs. For consistency purposes, our mantra is to run the 'most trusted merchant in town' by 'being great at the basics'. This vision and mission is backed up by the following generic overarching objectives: 'always ensure a core range of materials is available' (availability), 'buy in numbers to keep down buying costs' (purchasing efficiency), 'leverage St Gobain's vertical supply chain first' (internal optimisation), 'base pricing on margin capture' (profit optimisation) and 'reduce transportation distance by leveraging local demand' (distribution effectiveness). The issue I face is bringing these objectives alive at individual branch level. Previously, I was used to applying a pretty consistent set of measures to my stores within Jewson but in Gibbs & Dandy, given the different product mixes in the stores, I have to get each one to come up with what I call *'situational objectives'*: encouraging the stores to 'think for themselves' if they are to be successful in their local micro-markets! Let me give you examples of two stores, both in different markets and specialisms:

- [Town A] 'Civils' Merchant – This store deals with civil contractors, specialising in road and building materials. In the past, their contracts have been national – but at a cost (in terms of freight and price margin). What I have worked on with the management team is the concept of 'bringing it back local' in order to enhance 'viability'. In addition I have focused them upon extending their

CONTINUED …

range to supply 'generalist' builders to improve their business mix (away from a pure reliance on 'civils').

- [Town B] 'Electricals' Merchant – This store has a local market specialism located with electricals but has different issues. The local vision for this store is 'converting sales' through 'pricing compliance'. Although the unit has been extremely successful in driving sales, it has failed to drive margins adequately. Within the sales team at the store, however, some salesmen have better sales and margins than others. The objective here is to learn from and imitate their best practice in the local market.

In broad terms, the branch-level objectives do tie back to the company ones but the point is this: in order to apply a clear direction in branches with distinctive local markets, I have to apply a local vision and *situational objectives* which fit! These get buy-in from the team and get us closer to customer needs.

THREE KEY 'VISIONING' QUESTIONS FOR AMS

1. Do you have a clear vision of where you want to 'get' your district to?
2. Is it clearly articulated and understood by your GMs?
3. Are the tactics underpinning your vision likely to get you there?!

SALES-LED SERVICE CULTURE

MUEs are 'people-centric' businesses involving multiple transactions with numerous customer 'touch points' with a high degree of staff–customer interaction. Ideally, branded MUEs display the following service-based attributes:

IDEAL MUE SERVICE MODEL

- **Brand service concept:** Clear statement of the 'functional' and 'emotional' principles underpinning the service offer

- **Service delivery system:** A chain of service/service cycle which 'fits' the service concept underpinned by appropriate hard and soft resources
- **Features of effective service systems:**
  - System simplicity and memorability (for delivery) i.e.
    - retail: smile, speak, serve, send-off happy!
    - hospitality: embrace a friend (welcome), discover the desire (establish customer needs), showtime (simultaneous delivery), feel the fun (check back) and smiling send-off (quick resolution and good bye)
  - Empowered service providers that deliver the promise, resolve problems 'on the spot', provide the personal touch and go the extra mile
  - Appropriate facilities/amenities, machinery, technology and resources ('the enablers') that facilitate smooth transactions
  - Consumer perception exceeds initial expectations (i.e. speed, quality, politeness, recovery, knowledge etc.)
  - Users become 'net promoters' and advocates of the business
  - Insight systems that capture the views of lapsed and 'non-users'.

All too often, service delivery systems are not fit for purpose. The reasons for breakdowns are invariably context-specific, although common reasons include:

COMMON SERVICE MALFUNCTIONS

- **Design/perceptual 'gaps':**
  - **concept–service delivery 'gap':** Mismatch between brand service concept positioning (e.g. premium) and service delivery system (e.g. lack of personal 'touches' and value-added stages)
  - **senior leadership 'gap':** In understanding between concept design/execution and consumer need; insufficient provision of resources (hard and soft) to fulfil 'promise'
- **Positive advocacy equation malfunction:** Positive advocacy in brands/formats is the outcome of customer satisfaction – where perceptions exceed expectations – a function of the perception

of value, incorporating: price, product quality, amenity and service. Where there is a perceived imbalance/'deadly combination' between price, standard of amenity, product quality *and* 'level of service', perceptions of value dissipate affecting overall customer satisfaction scores and, ultimately, propensity to positively advocate use/adoption!

- **Evolution:** Lack of developmental progression in response to changing customer needs and expectations (due to technological/competitive innovation)

- **Customer competency:** In some concepts (particularly value) and cultures (especially emerging markets), behaviours might be rude and provocative, calling into question the 'customer is always right' mantra. To be sure, there are customers who behave like 'kings' having been granted sovereign status by the brand owner (the so-called 'sovereign effect'), resulting in extreme issues for service providers (exacerbated by behind-the-counter statements such as 'the staff in this shop are empowered to give you great service'!). Other contemporary issues affecting customer competency include 'technological distraction' – the inhibition of service interactions by mobile technology, where customers' obsession with checking/using mobile gadgets disrupts service-delivery rhythms/processes!

- **Viral feedback:** Real-time web-based feedback can affect the visiting/purchasing intentions (both negatively and positively) of existing/potential users.

- **'Coalescence' and 'occasionality':** Customer groupings are rarely homogeneous – getting different user groups who are using the product at different/similar times is an art (especially in multi-entertainment venues etc.).

- **Service provider needs/expectations/capability/profiles:** 'Point of service' operatives 'don't know', 'can't do' or (worse) 'don't care'! Staff are not homogeneous: 'balancers' (work–life), careerists (ambitious), social seekers (relational), advocates (believers), pragmatics (there for cash!).

- **Misaligned HRM systems:** Lack of aligned reward and two-way feedback mechanisms.

In spite of the above, the AM should be the 'cheerleader' and 'living embodiment' of his or her brand's service delivery system. Effective AMs drive sales-led service culture as follows:

HOW AMS DRIVE A SALES-LED SERVICE CULTURE

- **Customer obsessed:**
  - Always seeing the business from the customer's point of view; listening to feedback (quantitative and qualitative) and watching customer behaviour
  - Taking a 'one customer' approach where every interaction is seen as a valuable opportunity to build 'lifetime customer value'
  - Constantly reviewing the reasons behind 'walkouts', 'non-returns' and 'non-users' (sift through 'intellectual alibis' to understand deep-seated sub-conscious feelings and perceptions)
  - 'Leading the line' through:
    - impromptu stump speeches and pre-session huddle briefings
    - 'back to the floor' immersion and sales-led service modelling
    - removing toxic 'energy sappers' from the team quickly!

- **Supporting service providers through:**
  - Ensuring the cultural environment of the units is 'right':
    - outstanding customer-focused unit/shift leadership (behaviours and capabilities)
    - operational excellence (i.e. systems and standards adherence) which frees up capacity/underpins outstanding service execution
    - a complete understanding of roles and responsibilities
  - Making sure service providers are 'equipped' through:
    - right 'on the job' mindset (mood management techniques)
    - service delivery system training (immersion and refresher)
    - complaint-handling training (especially immediate rectification)
    - appropriate resources to do the job
  - Allowing some self-expression and autonomy:
    - a 'signature' expression or act that adds value to the service cycle

- ownership of one element of the cycle that the team member is an 'expert' upon and trains out to others
- Rewarding and celebrating success:
  - recognising individual/collective teamship WOW moments
  - swiftly celebrating instant 'defect recoveries' and 'going the extra mile'.

Case Study 4: Embedding a Guest-focused Culture in Innventure

Chris Gerard is the multi-site owner–entrepreneur of Innventure, an award-winning collection of premium pub restaurants. Previously an operational director, Chris built and ran some of the UK's largest pub restaurant chains (Vintage Inns, Harvester, Toby Carveries etc.).

... I believe that our present sales and profit success stems, in large part – alongside product quality and high standards of amenity – from the fact that we have built a guest-focused hospitality culture where our people (operating within a premium full-table-service concept) have built, *and* build, strong relationships with their customers. How have we built this front-line guest obsession? ... Obviously with systems and processes but also with vision and reward at the team-member level:

- *Service delivery system*: Our system is built around 'conductors' (two are used when we are 'full on') and a finely tuned 'orchestra' equipped with the right instruments and technical ability.
  - Conductors (co-ordinator and expeditor): Each busy trading session is overseen by two hosts (usually the managing partner, deputy and/or assistant) one of whom is a 'co-ordinator' overseeing smooth operation of the 'door', bar and table turn process backed up by an 'expeditor' managing the interaction between kitchen production and floor service.
  - Orchestra (order takers and runners): A few years ago we operated the archetypal 'section' management system where a designated waitress oversaw a defined section

CONTINUED ...

(i.e. number of tables) taking orders, carrying plates/drinks, securing payment and clearing down. What we do now is have two clearly defined roles, order takers and runners. Order takers concentrate solely on building relationships with their customers – discovering their needs and offering knowledge-based advice. Runners fulfil a more transactional role, delivering and clearing etc. Our order takers really are the key people in the business: these are the people that are passionate about the product, they really get it and they want to share their excitement about the offer with the guest. This has a number of critical benefits not least of which is that no inexperienced team member is order taking and the solution is also inherently more efficient, as it flexes more easily in terms of staggered rota starts than section operating allows.

- *Recruitment/selection*: We recruit people into the business who are (literally and metaphorically) 'sons and daughters of our guests'... essentially their profiles reflect our customer base, enabling them to understand aspirations, wants, desires and expectations... this furnishes them with the emotional capacity to read and react to our guests' needs and, with good fortune, ahead of the guest realising what those needs are. These new team members come to us pre-grounded by their parents!

- *Training*: We concentrate on what could be called hygiene and relationship training:

  - 'Hygiene': During induction our staff are trained in the basics (safe/secure, service steps, plate management, order taking/delivery etc.), essentially what a good job looks like and how this is measured.

  - 'Relationship': We work really hard to create an ambition, a vision, within our service providers, by describing what the key 'moments of truth' are for our customers and how these are personally realised by the individual team member. We explain to them that our guests aren't really dining at 'The Wellington', they are having dinner 'with Rebecca'! We educate them about the product through sampling (why rib eye is better than fillet, how our artisan chips are made, what wine is best with which dish etc.) and encourage them to

CONTINUED ...

'get closer, to interact warmly with customers' – 'owning the experience'. I can say unequivocally that our order takers really 'buy into' what we are doing; they are passionate about our product and know why it is good for the customer (both in terms of quality and value). This creates great customer relationships!

- *Reward*: Crucially, order takers keep their tips and tip in to their service providers. This serves as an instant reward for their discretionary effort and their levels of customer engagement. It also means that these roles are highly prized within the units; staff starting off behind the bar, or as runners, aspire to these positions. Also, order takers – if they are really successful – will always be motivated to work on key 'peak' shifts, meaning that our 'A Team' is always matched to the busiest sessions. Order taking in our businesses is seen as a prized privilege!

- *Pre-shift briefings*: Unlike the US, where the base cost of labour is low compared to the UK, it is impossible to schedule pre-session 'huddles' or 'buzz briefs'. For economic efficiency purposes, we have staggered shift patterns according to demand. This means that order takers and runners can enter the session at different timeslots – so how do we focus shift objectives? Line management will obviously play a role but the system we have in place is a simple clipboard that staff read prior to service, detailing who's on (the rota), daily specials, what went wrong/well in the last session and which products require 'selling through' quickly to minimise wastage (winners being offered a bottle of wine).

- *Service measurement*: Our customers are invited to fill in a 'stop, start, continue' feedback postcard, the results of which are communicated back to staff every couple of weeks in the exact same 'stop, start, continue' format. Also, we take comments from digital-media forums such as TripAdvisor extremely seriously – at first we might have been a little hesitant about its effect but we have listened and it has added value as a forum for feedback and insights. Finally, all is measured by a mystery diner programme, the results of which are highly visible across the company and fund the teams' Christmas party (or not!) depending on the teams' scores!

THREE KEY 'SALES-LED SERVICE' QUESTIONS FOR AMS

1. Do YOU take a CUSTOMER FIRST approach in everything you do?
2. Are your people sufficiently resourced and empowered to IMMEDIATELY RECTIFY service malfunctions?
3. Do you reward/recognise outstanding service behaviour?

TALENT ATTRACTION AND DEVELOPMENT

Proactively matching talent within the portfolio, ensuring that the 'the right GM is appointed to the right site at the right time' is the most important role of the AM. The main challenge posed by attempting to fit the right unit manager to the appropriate site lies in the sheer complexity of the exercise. Within their portfolio of sites, AMs will have a variety of units with specific traits: some might be newly invested (posing particular problems in changes of customer mix and systems design), others will have larger/smaller sales/ staff profiles and/or specific issues relating to safety, pilfering and non-standard layout and flows. *No one store or unit is exactly the same as any other*; a number of contextual factors need to be taken into account when making appointments for optimal fit between manager and site:

DIMENSIONS OF GM 'FIT'

- **Sectoral/domain fit**
  - Is this GM temperamentally suited to a B2C environment? Does this candidate have a 'happy' service-orientated personality i.e. does (s)he derive pleasure from serving/'doing things' for others?!
- **Organisational/brand fit**
  - Does this GM have a value set that chimes with those of the organisation/brand?
  - Will this GM fit the culture of the organisation/brand?
- **AM fit**
  - Can I work with this person? Will we mesh or mash! Will (s)he irritate me! Do we have any personal chemistry?
  - Is this GM capable of value-added followership i.e. is (s)he

reliable, tolerant (of my behaviour!), flexible, a critical thinker, open to learning and development etc.?

- **Job fit**
  - **Behavioural**
    - *Intrinsic motivation:* Does this GM have appropriate *needs and expectations* that will be fulfilled by the job role itself? Is s(he) realistic about the constraints surrounding the job but feels intrinsically motivated by the challenges and opportunities of leading a team of service providers?
    - *Team leadership:* Does s(he) have the capability to select, motivate and lead a team/sections of service providers, especially in units with a small management structure?
    - *Customer service:* Does s(he) have positive/happy social and interpersonal skills backed up with a real passion for satisfying customer needs? Is this person capable of going 'the extra mile', generating *memorable experiences* for customers (especially in hospitality where intangible memories – rather than tangible goods – are often all the customer leaves with!)
- **Technical**
  - *Numeracy:* Given the fact that performance is measured through financial metrics and tracked through key data reports is (s)he financially literate? Moreover can (s)he 'read the dependencies' between the P&L and other 'input metrics'?
  - *Administrative/managerial:* Does (s)he have adequate managerial and administrative skills in order to apply/ monitor blueprinted systems and processes?
  - *Technical/craft:* Does (s)he have craft (such as food production in casual dining), merchanting (layout and display) and/or technical (volume and capacity management) skills that will enable greater efficiency and effectiveness?
- **Cognitive**
  - *Thinking*: does (s)he have the ability to interpret and critically analyse quantitative and qualitative data in order to take remedial action?
- **Site fit**
  - **Demographic fit**: Does this GM fit with the customer profile in this particular location?

- **Family fit**: Does this site fit with the requirements/expectations of the GM's partner/family?
- **Store lifecycle fit**:
  - *Growth (investment)*: Does the GM have the required level of energy and passion to leverage the store through a high growth drive?
  - *Maturity*: Is the GM suited to sustaining the store through a period of under-investment and 'milking'?
  - *Turnaround*: Does the GM have the resilience, experience and/or drive to transform an underperforming site?
  - *Start-up:* Does the GM have the capability to deal with the uncertainty, ambiguity and fluidity of a start-up situation?
- **Team fit**
  - In addition to attitude and aptitude at an individual level, contributing to the wider team is important, with AMs asking themselves two questions:
    - Will this appointment improve the balance of skills, personalities and capabilities within my team?
    - Will this appointment infuse the team with more energy and drive?

But how do AMs ensure optimal 'fit'? It is essential, prior to appointment, that the AM assesses the technical, behavioural and cognitive sales-led service capabilities of the potential GM through a number of lenses:

HOW TO ASSESS GM 'FIT'

- **CV experience**
  - Technical/service skills (see above)
  - Domain knowledge
- **Interviews (CARR)**
  - Challenge: Describe a particular challenge/situation you faced trying to grow sales.
  - Action: What actions did you take to overcome this particular challenge?
  - Result: What were the sales outcomes of your actions?
  - Review: What did you learn from this process? What would you do differently?

- **Psychometric tests**
  - Service personality: Myers–Briggs, SHT
  - Resilience: MTQ48
- **Cognitive reasoning tests**
  - Verbal (interpretation), numerical (patterns and dependencies), problem-solving case studies
- **Observation**
  - Assessment centre group exercises
  - Trial assessment.

Poor assessment of 'fit' involves accepting ingratiation over expertise and qualifications, a failure to acknowledge genuine humility and declaration of weaknesses by candidates as a positive attribute, and ignoring signs of evasiveness (implausible claims, long-winded answers and conversing in impersonal tones).

Inevitably, it helps if the AM has engaged in proper talent and succession planning in order to build a pipeline of candidates within the portfolio to address talent gaps and forced/voluntary departures. This is invariably achieved through a proper review of requirements, 'gaps' and then remedial actions:

HOW TO PLAN FOR TALENT GAPS

- **WHAT do I need?**
  - Technical/behavioural/cognitive skills ('right person, right job, right place, right site, right time'?!)
  - Succession plan that *will improve* performance as 'gaps' appear
- **WHAT is the capability gap?**
  - **Performance:** What is the current performance of my key people?
  - **Potential:** What is the latent potential of my key people?
  - **Interventions:** Skills improvements/interventions to improve performance?
  - **Vacancies:** Where are vacancies most likely to occur (forced/unforced)?
- **WHAT do I need to do?**

- **Focus:** Spend at least 25% of my time on talent and succession planning
- **Act:** Put time and energy into those that 'can't do but care' rather than those that 'can do but don't care'!
- **Level:** Get involved in recruiting/assessing key people beneath GM, hold quarterly district meetings, mentor the outstanding talent
- **Search:** Look internally and externally for great people.

Given the inevitable scarcity of great people, building from within is a key role of the AM which is greatly assisted through professional development (PDP) meetings that examine performance, remedial actions and associated development interventions.

HOW TO CONDUCT A PDP

- **Review performance**
  - Metrics: Operational (sales, profit, margin, labour, standards/safety audit performance etc.), employee (t/o, engagement, succession planning) and customer (service satisfaction, complaints)
  - Remedial actions: Assess gaps against targets, consider dependencies and linkages (inputs/outputs), discuss actions
- **Development interventions**
- Consider performance, personality, capability, attitude, profile *and* organisational situation then choose between:
  - Technical/managerial development
    - Company courses, house of excellence training, 'sitting with Nellie', HR 'on the job' field training, process expert appointment
  - Behavioural/leadership skills
    - Observation & feedback, one-to-one coaching, 360 feedback, resilience training, mentoring, cluster lead appointment
  - Cognitive/thinking skills
    - Educational courses, projects, reflective diary, problem-solving exercises, critical thinking courses

Case Study 5: GM–Site 'Fit' in Sainsbury's

Tim Elliot (pseudonym) is the Regional Operations Manager for 21 units with Sainsbury's (over 1,000 stores).

... To my mind, fitting the right person to the site is one of the most important jobs I do... I have a range of units that vary in size from 30 to 60k sq ft, the amount of colleagues (200–500), size of management teams, range of demographic areas and locations – out of town, in town and suburban. Also, the stores are in different phases of their investment cycles – one of my main tasks is to ensure that any major refurbishments maximise their investment and, in the case of new openings, the stores set off in the right direction, with the right culture and performance trajectory; once a culture in a store is set, it is very difficult to shift! I can give you three recent examples...

[Refurbishment Fit] In the first case, when I took over the patch a year and a half ago, I knew that one of my stores (which accounts for 10% of the overall sales in my area) would be undergoing a multi-million-pound investment, increasing its size by nearly 30% to increase the general merchandise and clothing area. The store manager who was in place had been appointed by my predecessor, having followed in an extremely popular GM. This GM, unlike the one he had followed in, lacked buy-in and followership in the store. Colleagues complained that he was rarely seen on the floor and seemed to 'hide away' in his office. Staff pick up on messages from the GM pretty quickly: if the GM is in a bad mood or is invisible, morale throughout the store can change quite dramatically! Consequently, standards were not where I wanted them to be, units were uncared for and random rubbish seemed scattered about every time I came in. The mystery customer and availability scores of this store were not where I wanted them to be.

So what I did was bring his personal development review forwards and be completely honest with him: 'this is how the previous ROM viewed you, but I think you are in the "underachieving" box'. I also followed up with lots of one-to-ones and 'visits with a purpose'

CONTINUED ...

to put him on the right track. The upshot was that he decided to leave the company and work for one of our competitors. This enabled me to appoint a GM from a store nearby, who is a great leader, to oversee the 36-week refurbishment cycle. He managed it with great success: sales disruption figures were managed to target and excellent mystery customer (+8%) and availability (+1.5%) scores were maintained throughout. The new GM fits the culture of the store, is visible, has great leadership skills and colleague satisfaction is very high! I dread to think what might have happened if the previous GM had handled this project!

[Team Fit] In the second case, in another one of my stores the GM was convinced that just concentrating on the process would deliver the numbers. Her standards and service numbers were down, she was unhappy and was still talking to her ex-ROM. Again, I marked her as an 'under achiever' in her review and made a number of 'visits with a purpose'. On one of these visits I said 'what do you need from me?' She surprised me when she said that she wanted a new management team: she had found it difficult to change the old culture in the store with the team she currently had in place. So we took her deputy out (moving him to a different store) and put an experienced, 'softer' new one in. This broke up the clique beneath her and the team, under a new approach, has blossomed. They have come from the bottom to fourth or fifth on their cost controls, standards and service. The balance of the management team is now great. She got a great review from me last time out.

[Turnaround Fit] In the last case, I had a store that had become vacant with really poor metrics across the board. Usually, you might put in one of your 'rising star' deputies but I decided it needed real experience. Turning it around would really improve my district figures. I convinced one of my experienced guys to move in – this was a great turnaround opportunity for him that would enhance his profile and reputation. On the face of it, it wasn't a great move for him but the turnaround has been immense – he is happy, the store has really added to the overall performance of my area and the move has been a real success! …

THREE KEY 'TALENT ATTRACTION AND DEVELOPMENT' QUESTIONS FOR AMS

1. Do your GMs and their teams have 'service personalities'? (I.e. do they thrive on meeting customer needs?)

2. Are you deploying GM talent AND (simultaneously) developing your district 'bench strength' for future anticipated requirements? (Make sure you spend more time than you think you need on talent deployment and development – service-based businesses are all about people!!)

3. Are your PDP (personal development plan) meetings with your people HONEST and impactful?

TEAM WORKING AND MEETINGS

Another means by which AMs gain commitment and buy-in is through the active encouragement of cross-portfolio team working which yields reciprocity and mutual gain. Given the geographically isolated nature of many of their units, encouraging local team working reduces the psychological and physical burden, promising immense dividends in terms of morale and productivity. Effective AMs recognise that 'the whole is greater than the sum of its parts'; that by getting their team (in particular their unit managers) to work together, the general performance of their district will improve. Decreasing levels of 'social loafing' (i.e. 'hiding within the group') and encouraging high levels of interaction and 'sharing' are desirable particularly with regards to training and development (see above) and knowledge diffusion and process improvement. However, how do AMs create effective team working? How do organisations help them to do so and what are the barriers commonly confronted by AMs?

Starting with barriers, there are three main issues that impede successful team working across portfolios in MUEs, including:

BARRIERS TO TEAM WORKING

- **Architectural imprecision**: The poor structural design of the configuration of districts within organisations can hinder team working. Often due to secondary segmentation of the property portfolio (where units are split into new formats/old formats, core/non-core, approximations to certain sizes etc.), AMs might be designated large territories, overlapping their colleagues.

- **Self-interest**: The fact that all units are measured independently means that some unit managers might be unwilling to act in a co-operative fashion because they believe that, by swapping 'soft' or 'hard' assets, they might be helping their direct competition. Thus, whilst they might outwardly declare allegiance to the group, they act in a 'social loafing' manner!

- **Culture**: In some *power* cultures where the leader is expected to provide certainty and all the answers, members might be insufficiently socialised to work in autonomous teams.

Given these impediments, how do MUEs facilitate portfolio team working and what techniques do AMs deploy in order to facilitate their success?

FACILITATORS TO TEAM WORKING

- **Architecture**: At an organisational level, managing and/or regional directors will pay very close attention to the architecture of their districts to optimise AM efficiency and will also keep annual boundary reorganisations to a minimum in order to preserve relationships and tacit local knowledge. Also, companies need to judge carefully whether optimal performance is derived from controlling the 'same' type of outlet over a (potentially) vast geography or a 'mixed bag' of units in a tight territory. The downside of the former state is that time gets wasted travelling between units and there are difficulties building a tight team; whereas in the latter state, there is the difficulty of handling formats and addressing different channels that are serviced with different products, promotions, merchandising, customers etc.

- **Technology**: In some organisations, provision will be made for technology-enabled interfaces/interactions between AM and unit manager, and unit manager and unit manager (telephone conference facilities, Skype, web-cam, streaming etc.) to eliminate travel and movement offsite.

- **Incentives**: Other MUEs actively encourage teamwork through PRP mechanisms such as 'contribution' payments (an annual payment of up to 10–20% of base salary) which are based upon the AM's assessment of their unit manager's overall added value input to the wider team and general portfolio performance.

- **Team meetings:** In terms of team meeting structures, some organisations also mandate the numbers and types of meetings that should take place at district (i.e. monthly district meetings with prescribed agendas that fit with normal internal communication/briefings cycles and weekly business tele-conference calls) and unit level (i.e. daily 'buzz' briefings, end-of-shift meetings, weekly action meetings, monthly strategy meetings etc.).

Given the importance of meetings to building cross-portfolio team working, how should AMs hold their weekly/monthly meetings and how should they conduct themselves?

HOW TO HOLD TEAM MEETINGS

- **Weekly conference/Skype calls** (short-term focus)
  - Operate according to a set agenda backed up with standardised reportage
  - Review 'dashboard' performance against objectives (sales, labour, service, costs etc.)
  - Review 'league table' absolute and relative performance
  - Request progress updates on focus areas, initiatives and projects
  - Agree further 'improvement' actions and timescales
  - Despatch 'what, when and whom' e-mail
- **Monthly district meetings** (long-term focus)
  - **Venue** – select different store locations for learning opportunities
  - **Agenda**
    - consistent structure; built around 'local vision' and objectives
    - short review of the past; majority of items 'forward looking'
    - 'bite-sized chunk' agenda items
  - **Theme**
    - local priority (i.e. 'crushing costs', 'driving sales penetration', 'growing NPS service scores', 'bringing on talent' etc.) or…
    - upcoming seasonal event (range change, Xmas etc.) or…

- company-wide initiative (new launch, restructure etc.)
- **Attendees** – invite GMs, members of the wider team and head office 'experts', 'friends' and 'advisors'
- **Materials/handouts** – professionally crafted; standard format
- **Presenters/delivery** – include 'cluster leads', 'process champions'; encourage multi-media delivery, charts and pictures rather than just words and numbers!
- **Insight capture** – appoint 'flight controller' who captures 'tankbuster' insights/actions from the group
- **Prizes/competitions** – present awards to winners of district competitions (margin control, service, sales etc.)
- **Feedback** – capture anonymous feedback on meeting by form at the end of the meeting
- **Evening 'bonding'** – organise an evening event which will enable members of the team *and* support functions to build social and relational capital
- **Follow up** – minutes, correspondence and action-lists must be short, to the point with 'by whom', 'by when' referencing

HOW TO BEHAVE IN MEETINGS

- **AMs must:**
  - Be authentic
  - Overcome objections through listening, empathising, then moving onto solutions/positives!
  - Agree behavioural 'rules of conduct'/'group contract' with the team:
    - act with maturity, leave egos outside the door, listen with respect, fully contribute, focus on solutions rather than problems, always on time, smartly dressed
  - Co-opt the 'big dogs' (opinion formers) on important issues before the meeting... but always listen to the quietest voice in the meeting
  - Encourage *all* participants to share best practice and insights (prevent 'social loafing'!)
  - Constantly beware of the (ever present) danger of the 'irrationality of group decision making' and *'polarised positions'*

(i.e. being in a group can exaggerate members' opinions, causing them to make more extreme decisions/suggestions)

- **AMs must avoid:**
  - Pretending to know all the answers
  - Overpromising and under delivering
  - Declaring victory too soon
  - Negativity and 'bad mouthing' (i.e. the centre/other districts)
  - Focusing upon 'uncontrollables'
  - Information overload and excessive compliance focus
  - An exclusively short-term focus
  - Just telling rather than listening and involving

Case Study 6: Utilising the Team in Loungers

Until February 2014, Alex Marsh was an operations manager for Loungers (responsible for 11 units), a fast-growing informal restaurant bar chain that caters to urban professionals and their families. He now combines a smaller field-based role for Loungers in addition to responsibilities for operational excellence. After an early career in law, Alex has worked extensively in premium food service, opening over 20 sites for Loungers, Blubeckers and the Premium Country Dining Group.

... Having been both GM and AM for Loungers during a period of rapid growth, I recognise and am a strong advocate of using the 'talents of all the team' to improve our capability/capacity... Yes, we have meetings where ideas are swapped, a collegiate atmosphere is generated and participants depart with a sense of direction/ purpose but the way in which I engender 'teamship' is through close interaction between units at a local or cluster level... A tight sense of togetherness is essential given our roll-out plans... Last year, for instance we opened thirteen units and we could only have achieved this by using what I call the 'brains trust' of the area... I have nominated experts who, after detailed planning on my part,

CONTINUED ...

handle the various elements of the pre-opening process... One of my GMs works closely with me recruiting the new site GM, assistant, head chef, and sous chef... [T]hese key figures (if they have come from outside the company) are then immersed in the company, rotating around units for hands-on practical training in all aspects of our operation... Then, pre-opening training is handled by different GMs who are outstanding in various areas: compliance/safety, floor service and cocktail/coffee training for instance... with food production being taught by two chefs: one who has a real talent for administration/preparation and another who is a superb cook... all are enthusiastic and passionate about their areas of expertise...

My philosophy is that keeping things local is best... best-practice training and the swapping of people/resources is best done locally rather than centrally... One of the main by-products of this is that managers and staff from different sites in my area create *close* bonds between one another... This is what creates a real team at portfolio level... people like helping others because it makes them feel good – it raises their sense of self-esteem... It also keeps them close to the customer and local community... GMs/head chefs from one site, having covered for, trained and worked in other sites, get to know their staff and customers... This gives them insight into other businesses but also creates trust, understanding and mutual respect... The people in this business are taught to be mobile, agile and flexible... It is not just about *their* site or *their* people; it is about the wider area and business... the contribution they can make... (*Do you incentivise people for this behaviour?*) ... Not through cash – you don't need to... For these behaviours (which I demonstrate myself) we celebrate through giving out ad hoc gifts (premium knives to head chefs!), going for fun days out and covering units to let all the staff have a fun night out... We are one team on this area... every job is important as the other... helping one another out makes us all stronger, happier!

THREE KEY 'TEAM WORKING AND MEETINGS' QUESTIONS FOR AMS

1. Have you 'set up' your district to work together effectively and interact as a team?
2. Are your meetings properly scheduled, well planned (with clear objectives) and INCLUSIVE?
3. Reflect on your behaviour during meetings – is it authentic? (I.e. don't try and be somebody you're not – admit that you don't know everything – use all the talents!)

TRUST AND RECOGNITION

Thus far, some of the practices elucidated above have touched upon the need for AMs to create a climate of trust and recognise superior performance in order to create a high-performance environment. Building trust is crucial in bolstering human relations – generally portrayed as the extent to which one party *believes* that another party will act both *transparently* and *consistently* in a fair, honest and benevolent manner. Its benefits include greater predictability of social life, community cohesion and a more effective working environment that enables members to work together. Breaches of trust can degrade relationships, although they might be forgiven if they arise through a lack of competence or are followed by immediate admission/recovery. Trust builds confidence and followership, with consistent behaviours and honest communications between parties forming a key part of the equation. With regards to behaviours, trust can be built by AMs in the following manner:

HOW AMS BUILD TRUST

- Consistent behaviour (explain decisions)
- Yes means yes – no means no!
- Delivering on promises (spontaneous favours create powerful needs to reciprocate!)
- Protection from punishment (where merited)
- Loyalty to staff in front of 'outsiders'
- No negative 'toilet talk'
- Avoidance of mixed messaging

- Openness, honesty and truthfulness
- Demonstration of humility (avoid 'When I did...'; admit 'I don't know!')
- 'Pratfalls' (i.e. committing blunders) will increase likability and authenticity!
- Relentless focus upon sales growth (signals job security)
- Judicious use of positional power.

HOW AMS UNDERMINE TRUST

- Inappropriate relationships
- Using staff as 'emotional crutches'
- Excessive favouritism (particularly to poor performers)
- Overpromising, under delivering
- Nakedly self-interested behaviour
- Immature indiscretion (this leads to *spontaneous trait transference* where listeners will unconsciously associate the AM with the characteristics they are describing!)
- Ego, narcissism, hubris!

Inevitably communication plays a big part in building trust between AMs and their followers, with AMs paying particular attention to process, content and follow-up:

HOW TO BUILD TRUST THROUGH COMMUNICATIONS

- **Process**: AMs will engage *directly* with their followers through multiple media (telephony, digital etc.) although face-to-face meetings remain the most powerful mechanisms (i.e. reviews, 'visits with a purpose', district meetings etc.)
- **Content**: AMs ensure that the content of their communications is honest, transparent, jargon free, simple and consistent
- **Follow up**: Communications are *followed up* with hard, visible outputs.

Trust is reinforced by the extent to which AMs recognise and positively reinforce good performance and high levels of discretionary effort. Research has consistently shown that expressing a sincere interest in others through listening and asking personal questions – combined with ensuring that positive remarks outweigh negative ones by at least a 5:1 ratio – lead to good relationships, reciprocation and indebtedness. Effective AMs are adept, whatever the prevailing climate, at creating emotional buy-in through planned and spontaneous recognition at all levels throughout their portfolio.

HOW DO AMS RECOGNISE PERFORMANCE

- **Formal**
  - Nominations for awards at district, regional or company level (staff member of the year, store of the year, manager of the year etc.)
  - 'Winner' or best-practice citations in round-robin e-mails, newsletters, district meetings
- **Informal**
  - Spontaneous phone calls to thank staff in person
  - Store visits – sometimes with notables (regional or operations director) – specifically designed to thank staff in person
  - Handwritten letters expressing personal gratitude

In addition, AMs show a 'personal touch outside of just work things', remembering birthdays, recognising notable events such as births and marriages and showing genuine compassion and pastoral care for staff during times of personal difficulty (granting time off without any quibbles). Displaying recognition or carrying out a favour will often result in followers giving something significantly bigger in return!

Case Study 7: Operational Line Reflections on Recognition, Trust and Reciprocation

Over the course of four academic years (2009–2013), over 400 unit and area managers have attended foundation and post-graduate degree courses in Multi-Unit Leadership and Strategy at BCBS.

Unlike some of the [area] managers I've had before, this one doesn't send out sinister district e-mails praising a few and then dumping on the rest by *highlighting people at the bottom of league tables in red!*... actually what he does is recognises how far some people have come on certain measures and praises improvement as well as top performance...

Unit Manager, Retail

My [area] manager is very good at picking the phone up to me and saying 'well done', particularly on Mondays after busy sessions over the weekend to give me a bit of a lift or after we've done something particularly good... like great sales, mystery customer or safety visits... unlike other managers I've had, I don't hear his voice and think 'here's another bollocking!'

General Manager, Hospitality

My [area] manager is good at remembering our birthdays and always delivers a present... a few bottles of wine or a tin of sweets at Xmas. It's a personal touch and we really appreciate it... Actually, we would walk over hot coals for him!

Unit Manager, Leisure

It is quite clear to us [area managers] that some of the rules and procedures fall into the 'business prevention' category but the audit team hammer the units if they don't comply when they come in and do their quarterly checks. What I do is tell my people to ignore some of the trivial box ticking and focus on what really matters – the customer. Anything that relates to selling more... creating a good customer experience in a safe environment will do for me... There

CONTINUED ...

have been times when I have gone to quite senior personnel to get some of these 'process jockeys' off my case... My team know I stick up for them and am trying to do the right thing, so (as a consequence) I think they trust me and therefore 'put more out' for me... I really do...

Area Manager, Retail

[T]o a certain extent, we are made to look like dicks on occasions because things hurtle down that we have no input into but can have quite bad effects... my people can look at me sometimes and think 'what power does he have!?' ... so the way in which I get people on-board is to cut a deal with them really... 'you concentrate on what is really important and I'll do my best to act as a shield against all the crap'... 'if somebody comes in for you I promise I will protect you – they will have to sack me before you!'... it is this, what I call – as the guy in the Fokkers film put it – the 'circle of trust' that keeps the show on the road! ... because my team knows that I will do everything to protect them from the centre, I can rely on them to do things for me 'quid pro quo'...

Area Manager, Hospitality

THREE KEY 'TRUST AND RECOGNITION' QUESTIONS FOR AMS

1. Reflect on your behaviour – is it honest and trustworthy?
2. Reflect on your decision making – is it consistent and reliable?
3. Do you regularly praise and recognise the achievements of both your direct and your wider team?

SUMMARY

This chapter began by considering briefly the meaning of generating commitment from an organisational level, concluding that its purpose was to increase engagement and discretionary effort (through techniques/practices such as leadership and HRM). However, Chapter 3 surfaced many of the issues faced by AMs, one of its main insights being that because of the distance of the centre and policy makers from the units, many policies/initiatives might be mistimed or unfit for purpose. Indeed, the survey highlighted in Figure 3.1 illustrated the mismatch between GM understanding/buy-in of the organisation's super-ordinate goals (low) compared to their buy-in to their local portfolio objectives (high). This would suggest that it is the effective AM's ability to reduce their own personal distance with their followers through a variety of practices and interventions that marks them out as being particularly effective.

But what are these interventions and what practical effects do they have upon reducing distance? Taking in turn the practices outlined above, first, the creation of a *local vision and clear direction* and deployment of relevant *recognition* mechanisms have the effect of reducing *structural distance* (both hierarchical and geographical) by achieving coherence, relevance and focus within the portfolio. Indeed, the Gibbs & Dandy case study supporting the insights in this section suggested that success in a 'soft branded' context could only be achieved through the shaping commitment towards 'situational objectives' at unit/portfolio level. Second, *psychological distance* between the AM, their followers and customers could only be reduced – in demographic and cultural terms – through the crafting of a relentless *sales-led service culture*. Thus, whatever the gaps between central policy makers and customers – their perception of the service concept/delivery system needed to satisfy customers and the actual expectations of customers themselves – the effective AM has a huge role in ensuring that their followers/service providers get 'up close and personal' with their customers (a point validated in the Innventure case study which advocated the recruitment of the 'sons and daughters' of their customers!) Closing psychological distance with customers is further reinforced by appropriate *talent attraction and fit.* Finally, however, there is a *functional* dimension to the closure of distance, with effective AMs integrating and involving 'outsider' support functions into their district meetings and – from a vocational (job/roles) point of view – gaining an appreciation of 'what their people do' by constantly refreshing their technical skills by '*training the trainers*' and 'back to the floor' experiences.

However, closing down *structural*, *psychological* and *functional* forms of **distance** within the portfolio through commitment-led practices is extremely time intensive, requiring a high level of energy/emotional intelligence 'expenditure' from the effective AM! Thus, in order to decrease levels of detachment, isolation and non-alignment through high levels of local leadership, the effective AM must also exert 'operational grip' in order to create **capacity** for action. These elements of AM practice will be elucidated in the next chapter.

CONTROL

The central premise of multi-unit enterprises (MUEs) is dependability and consistency – hence the crucial importance of the area manager (AM) in ensuring rigorous conformity to pre-set processes and standards. This has been a cornerstone element of the role since its genesis from 'store super-visor' in the late nineteenth century, when AMs were principally deployed in the field to 'check' and 'police' head-office policy and practice adherence at unit level. With the onset of computers and other digital technology, many of the menial tasks carried out by AMs – checking paper-based weekly sale of business (WSOB) ledgers, cash handling/banking systems and stock availability – have been automated, granting head office real-time information and direct 'management through the wire'. The fact remains, however, that there is a plethora of processes, standards and systems in MUEs which are connected to the effective delivery of the product offer, and which the AM is expected to monitor and regulate in order to ensure operational excellence.

The problems that AMs face in expediting conformance and order were referred to at the end of Chapter 3, not least the degree of rules/metric overload that exists in many MUEs and the problems of *physical* distance that limit the AMs' *'capacity to act'*. So alongside generating commitment, discussed earlier, which will reduce levels of psychological distance and stimulate high degrees of motivation and discretionary effort, how do AMs ensure *'operational grip'* in their portfolios which will increase their *capacity to add value?* Further, which elements of AM professional practice are vital for the expedition of the role? This chapter considers these questions first by understanding the nature of control from both an academic and AM perspective, and second by reviewing prescribed AM practices which focus upon ensuring execution of many of the facets of operational excel-lence outlined in Chapter 3, for example: blueprint mastery, values and intentional behaviour, planning and prioritisation, monitoring and correction, delegation and networking, and autonomy and deviance (giving up control to gain control!)

UNDERSTANDING CONTROL

ACADEMIC COMMENTARY

The term 'organisation' implies a structural form whose central purpose is to control and coordinate activities to ensure maximum efficiency. Characteristic of most organisations, therefore, is the underlying purpose of control, the assumption being that the imposition of *consistency* and *order* will produce *measurable* and *dependable outcomes*. According to Tannenbaum, one of the most eminent scholars to have commentated on this area:

> Organisations require a certain amount of conformity as well as the integration of diverse activities. It is the function of control to bring conformance to organisational requirements and the achievement of the ultimate purposes of the organisation...

(1968: 3)

In normative terms, the prescription of processes, tasks, roles and reward systems is designed to achieve simultaneously both alignment and control. As managers seek certainty of outcome, the imposition of a series of interventions that facilitate control is seen to be preferable to its diametric alternative, anarchy.

In ideal conditions, effective control systems have a number of defining characteristics:

- *Simplicity*: Management control systems work when they are simple, visible and easily understood by all workers within the organisation.
- *Alignment*: Processes and controls produce assured outcomes when they are aligned with the structure, culture and vital activities of the organisation, connecting with key strategic objectives and functional decision centres.

- *Correction*: Control systems that work signal deviation, malfunction and adverse performance quickly and clearly to decision makers, affording corrective action.

- *Adaptability*: Whilst being accurate, timely and dependable, management control systems should be adaptable and subject to continuous improvement and review.

It is acknowledged, however, that levels and types of control are contingent upon a number of intervening variables. Organisational maturity, economic conditions, industry, culture and leadership have all been cited by commentators as having an effect on the form and nature of control. For instance, Child's (1988) typologies of control – ranging from loose to tight – are heavily influenced by sector and nature of work processes (i.e. variable or repetitive):

- *Loose controls*: Professional organisations (such as solicitors and management accountants) are characterised by *loose* and fluid 'cultural control' systems due to the variety of their work.

- *Tight controls*: SMEs have high levels of 'personalised central control' where the proprietor keeps very *tight* control on tasks and activities.

- *Hybrid*: In MUEs, contingent variables relating to control will include (in addition to the previously mentioned factors such as maturity, economic conditions etc.) the degree of branding (i.e. 'hard' or 'soft') and/or the level of customisation and localisation.

How desirable or beneficial is control? From an *individual perspective*, research has found that in certain circumstances workers actually accede to control systems, a state that Lawler (1976) ascribes to three reasons:

- *Feedback*: Most workers welcome feedback on their performance against prescribed rules and procedures to ensure that they are 'doing it right'.

- *Structure*: Staff prefer some semblance of task structure and order – as opposed to disorganisation – in order to calibrate their performance.

- *Reward*: In situations where pay is contingent on performance, workers are apt to accept control systems as a *cost* that can be outweighed by the financial *benefits* accruing from the coordinated organisation of their effort and labour.

At the *organisational level*, control is deemed beneficial from a scientific management perspective because discipline and order can be applied so as to ensure that tasks are executed on time, to standard, and for predictable and measurable outcomes. Thus control involving all the foundations of modern management – objective setting, planning, organising, directing, monitoring and reviewing – is desirable in order to direct the right behaviours to optimise organisational performance. However, whilst scientific management, exemplified through work processes such as 'Fordism' and 'Lean', has merits in terms of its emphasis upon central coordination and measurement of standardised and repetitive tasks, it falls short due to its lack of *worker autonomy* and *contribution to the decision-making process*, with all their attendant negative effects.

Critics of excessive control have four principal objections to both its desirability and sustainability:

- *Ethical*: From an ethical and moral standpoint, excessive control runs counter to the principles of individualistic Western liberal democracy.

- *Fear*: As control is fundamentally defined as regulating behaviour and, as such, rewards compliant behaviour whilst punishing misdemeanours, it can create fear and stress.

- *Inefficiency*: Because organisations are essentially a construction of complex webs of informal human interactions, only *limited* control can ever be achieved over work behaviour through control systems. In reality, a large proportion of work and behavioural control is achieved through informal negotiation, persuasion and manipulation rather than formal rules and procedures. Control regimes neglect the social needs, expectations and aspirations of workers. High levels of control can therefore result in high levels of inefficiency caused through workplace conflict, resistance and/or deviance.

- *Accountability*: Excessive control can negatively affect accountability, innovation, independent thinking and risk taking. Workers become 'drones' who obey hierarchical authority silently in exchange for job security and protection from punishment.

AMS AND CONTROL

Due to the structure, form and purpose of the standardised multi-unit organisation, there is inevitably a major focus on compliance and control due to geographical dispersion and the need for the centre to impose order (see Chapter 3). Thus it is an incontrovertible fact that MUEs need to deploy systemised and standardised ways of working which supply *assured and measurable outcomes* for all stakeholders.

AMs play a key role in monitoring and implementing many of the MUE's controls and initiatives, acting as a conduit between the head office and their units. At times, however, given the vast number of measures, tasks and ad hoc requests they have, MULs face information overload combined with a real fear of punishment and retribution if they fail to fulfil central dictats. This can result in immobilising levels of fear, stress and dissatisfaction. Coupled with the fact that they may be operating in regimes that deploy 'rhetoric' type HRM and where their senior executives might be playing power games in their privileged position as agents rather than stewards of the business, this may result in AMs being faced with seemingly intractable and insurmountable obstacles in exerting meaningful, sustainable control in some multi-unit contexts. How are AMs able to perform effectively in such hostile conditions?

Many commentators assume that prevailing company cultural climate, leadership and HRM practices frame general organisational performance; however, based on empirical observation and evidence, my research suggests that AMs can still make a significant difference to outcomes at unit level. As has been argued previously, each unit will have its own particular micro-market, local labour-supply characteristics and unique sub-culture based on previous local management styles and approaches. Given that in *uniformly* challenging contexts some AMs outperform others, it is self-evident that those who demonstrate better performance over a sustained period must be doing something more effectively than their peers. The previous chapters alluded to the specific commitment-based practices that AMs were apt to deploy. However, another feature is the degree to which effective AMs are able not only to generate commitment but also to ensure effective control.

The following sections will argue that effective AMs are able to facilitate control – adherence to measurement, rules and procedures, and acceptance of initiatives – through a number of practices. These mechanisms will now be considered in turn.

MONITORING AND CORRECTION

In order to provide consistency across their formats, all MUEs will provide their front-line operations with a blueprinted guide which provides information and instruction regarding how the product should be executed. Often this blueprint will cover a range of standard operating procedures (SOPs) relating to back-of-house (BOH) systems and processes relating to front-of-house (FOH) sales-led service execution (see Chapter 3). In terms of ensuring *'macro-adherence'* against its blueprint, MUEs will conduct planned or random checks to assess levels of adherence or deviation. In franchised contexts, the implications for non-conformance by franchisees (master, multiple or individual) to codified procedures can result in costs such as penalty charges or, in extreme circumstances, termination. Hence the importance of the role of the AM in ensuring *'micro-adherence'* to blueprinted standards and systems in franchised environments. But what are the issues confronting AMs in their local surveillance and application of the blueprint, and how do they overcome them?

There are a myriad of issues faced by AMs in executing the blueprint which can be classified as being *operational*, *cultural* and *personal*:

BARRIERS TO BLUEPRINT ENFORCEMENT

- **Operational**: From an *operational* point of view, how accurately has the blueprint been translated from its source (operations or marketing) and to what extent has it been adapted effectively to mirror local conditions? What resources have been supplied to the AM to ensure its effective execution – has the necessary capital and investment been supplied in order to enable conformance? Certainly, at times, AMs will find themselves at the point of delivery without the necessary physical and human wherewithal to fulfil the requirements outlined in the operational blueprint. How do they improvise in order to fulfil pre-ordained duties and tasks?

- **Cultural**: From a *cultural* perspective – in *high context* 'relational' environments where there is a reliance on spoken rather than written agreements, with concomitant gaps in capability around simple managerial functions such as checking, monitoring and measuring – AMs might struggle to get their unit personnel to understand and/or implement codified rules and procedures.

- **Personal**: From a personal perspective, in cultures with high levels of *power distance*, AMs might be apt to adopt a detached perspective due to their perceived levels of personal power (derived from their hierarchical status), meaning that they are insufficiently in control of what is happening on the ground because they have outsourced responsibility (under the aegis of punishment) to their front-line operatives.

Given these issues, how do effective AMs execute the blueprint? In many cases, AMs in MUEs, having been promoted from unit-manager level, will be familiar with the blueprinted detail; and having been promoted for (amongst other things) their technical competence, will be able fulfil the policing and checking aspects of their role effectively, due to prior knowledge and experience. However, it is the AM's ability to *manage at a distance* that marks them out as supreme operators.

HOW AMS ENFORCE THE BLUEPRINT

- **'Mastery' of the detail**: Effective AMs will understand most (if not all) of the vital systems and processes that lie behind the blueprint (either through prior experience as a GM or intensive training/back-to-the-floor activities).

- **'Visits with a purpose'**: Located off-site with multiple unit responsibility, AMs schedule spontaneous or mandatory/planned 'visits with a purpose' to conduct operational-excellence audits and due-diligence checks (see 'Planning and Organising' in Chapter 3). Generally store visits will be split so that two-thirds are formal (announced) and one-third unannounced. Formal visits will encompass operational audits, performance reviews/coaching and strategy meetings, whilst informal visits will include observation, monitoring, ad hoc/dummy audits and social/relational interaction.

- **Planning, organisation and action**: In order to be successful, AMs must adopt the *managerial practices* necessary to execute, namely: planning, scheduling, organising, delegating and 'chasing up' (see 'Planning and Organising' in Chapter 3). AMs in certain cultural contexts will assume that, given their elevated position 'above the units', they can abandon all accountability to unit level, stepping in only to punish non-conformance when it goes wrong. Successful AMs do not wait for system failure: they anticipate problems (usually through data analysis and observation) by adopting a *proactive* rather than *reactive* stance.

- **'Spreading the load'**: Effective AMs are also adept at using the resources of their organisation and district to act as additional 'eyes and ears':
  - *District level*: At a district level they might use some of their most capable unit managers to run 'interim' or 'dummy' audits to check on compliance, to provide their units with calibrated trial runs.
  - *Central resources*: Utilising other agencies within the organisation such as property and maintenance, HR and internal audit (such as stock takers) also helps 'spread the load' providing invaluable information on adherence.
- **Refusal 'to walk by'**: Although there are a myriad of auditing devices and standards manuals which will detail required systems execution and brand standards adherence, effective AMs will never 'walk by' or ignore things which patently are defective/wrong. In particular, anything that is a safety hazard will be confronted/addressed by the AM on the spot.

In most circumstances, AMs will take a 'mediating' approach to correction and enforcement – agreeing actions that need to be taken in advance of follow-up visits. In extreme, circumstances, however, where extreme breaches of the blueprint occur (particularly with regard to legal obligations or health and safety), the AM will have to take formal disciplinary action. Prior reference has been made to the fact that AMs must 'SEE AND SPEAK' as opposed to 'walking by' and letting things get out of hand; but when severe malfunctions occur the AM will have to take formal disciplinary action.

HOW TO CONDUCT FORMAL DISCIPLINARIES

- **Invitation**: Write to the recipient inviting them to a meeting, clearly stating the subject matter, its possible outcomes and (if necessary) allowance for accompanying representatives
- **Reason/criteria**: At the meeting clearly state the breach of company policy and/or area of underperformance against agreed criteria (state that minutes of the meeting will be taken)
- **Check understanding**: Check recipient understanding of 'the breach' and 'the rules/procedures'

- **Explanation**: Seek explanation for 'breach' (take detailed minutes)
- **Consideration**: Take time out to give serious consideration to the explanation and actions to be taken (if a satisfactory explanation is given, no further action is to be taken)
- **Reconvene meeting**: Give the recipient the adjudication outcome and its reasons
- **Issue formal warning**: Issue formal warning (verbal or written), state length of time on file and appeals procedure
- **Rectification**: Jointly agree a measurable improvement plan with associated training/guidance and future meeting dates

Case Study 8: Monitoring and Correction in Hungry Horse

David Stallard (PGDip MULS with distinction 2014) is an area manager (16 units) for Hungry Horse (200+ sites), one of the UKs fastest-growing mid-market family pub restaurant chains.

... The way in which I enforce the blueprint within my brand is to, first, have complete mastery and insight of its standards and systems; second, monitor its successful execution through analysing the data and making appropriate linkages; third, seek to evaluate problems on the ground through visits with a purpose; and fourth, take corrective action to ensure conformance and excellence:

- *Mastery*: As an ex-unit manager who has 'grown up' with the brand since its early days and an area manager of five years' standing, I am completely 'on top' of the systems and standards that underpin the blueprint. This is vital in assisting me to monitor adherence, locate breakdowns and administer corrective solutions.
- *Analysis and linkages:* I analyse my businesses in the following fashion:

CONTINUED ...

- P&L data: I analyse my house P&Ls for sales trends. Food-sales declines (particularly when coupled with liquor increases) are a particular cause for concern.

- Covers data: If food sales are down, rather than analysing spend-per-head (SPH) data – something that can be affected by seasonal and 'payday' factors – I will go straight to cover reports (i.e. numbers of meal transactions). A decline – particularly in light of the barnstorming success of Horse – is a real cause for concern.

- Food-quality data: In my experience, there will always be a link between cover decline and food quality. Looking at customer-service data will nearly always back up my hypothesis of a linkage.

- Day-by-week data: Also by looking at data by specific day slots, connections between peak periods such as Sundays, patterns of sales decline and food-quality collapses will tell me a lot about why covers aren't turning over the rest of the week!

- *Visits with a purpose*: Having analysed the data, what I tend to do is hit the 'big ticket' problems – the four or five outlets with sales-decline problems. What I do is make unannounced visits (most frequently on a Sunday) and order seven items off the menu and – with the food-specification sheets in front of us – taste them with the GM or deputy. I generally select staple dishes – roast, fish and chips, steak, pie etc. – and judge them on quality according to the spec. For instance, is the fish watery (indicating it has been run through tap water) or the batter peeling off (due to the age of the oil)? If the food is unacceptable, I book a return visit there and then.

- *Remedial action*: What I put in place before my return visit are calls from regional/area chefs, bespoke training courses and visits for the GM and/or KM to our Kitchens of Excellence. If after a couple more visits from me the food remains clearly unacceptable, I will go down a 'formal route' because the incumbent operator clearly has capability/conduct issues. I will send out a letter of invitation to a formal disciplinary but, frequently, given the help I have given to individuals, coupled with the pressure I

CONTINUED ...

have applied through successive visits with a purpose, the GM will decide to move on. As the process has unfolded, I have already made 'worst case' backfill contingency plans, so am normally able to move swiftly in the case of a vacancy. I must stress, however, that this happens infrequently and many has been the time that GMs have turned their performance around by really engaging with – and solving – food-quality issues by confronting people, process and product issues in the kitchen…

THREE KEY 'MONITORING AND CORRECTION' QUESTIONS FOR AMS

1. Do you ever 'walk by' serious standards/systems breaches? (You must 'SEE AND SPEAK'! – in both formal AND informal 'visits with a purpose'.)

2. Do you use 'all the talents' on the district to monitor and correct standards?

3. Do you make sure that you follow procedure (either by consulting HR or policy documents) to rectify serious breaches? (The financial/reputational costs of not doing so might be significant to the organisation!)

PRIORITISATION AND LINKAGES

Given the fact that many MUEs are derived from Anglo-American contexts, many organisations will rely on bureaucratic 'output controls' (Ouchi 1979, Jaeger 1983): a set of outcome-related measures that help 'controllers' and 'senior managers' in the firm to analyse and assess performance. In MUEs, these metrics will form part of a 'multi-layered net' within the operational line (Garvin and Levesque 2008) so that organisations have a line of sight on the despatching of key priorities. In some organisations, these outputs are coupled with inputs in the form of a balanced scorecard where *operational and financial outputs* are bound together with *people and customer-related inputs*. Such frameworks set clear parameters and expectations within the organisation whilst creating a high degree of alignment/congruence, often bolstered through associated reward and performance systems (typically more connected to 'hard' financial outputs rather than 'soft' people inputs). But what are the issues AMs face attempting to prioritise and how do they overcome them (perhaps through establishing linkages and targeted interventions)?

The issues facing AMs in prioritising outputs relate, again, to operational, cultural and personal factors:

BARRIERS TO PRIORITISING OUTPUTS

- **Operational**: Organisational priorities and targets might be poorly expressed, constantly changing or, as previously stated, over-emphasising 'hard' financial outputs to the detriment of all other measures. In addition, they might be insufficiently cognisant of the local environment, being a direct translation of what is more important in the national rather than the local market. Homogenous metrics that make sense at a strategic level might have little relevance or practicability at a micro-market level. How does the AM deal with this ambiguity and complexity?

- **Cultural**: In addition, from a cultural perspective, AMs might be operating in contexts with low levels of achievement orientation – due to a belief in 'pre-ordained' fatalism – and polychromic *temporal* characteristics which emphasise longer- rather than shorter-term time horizons (Hoftstede 1980, 1991, Scarborough 1998). How does the AM gain buy-in to short-term metrics and acceptance for the need to respond to urgent organisational priorities in these diffuse contexts?

- **Personal**: Also, from a *personal* point of view, given their cultural pre-programming and dispositions, AMs might either be fairly sanguine about the need to respond to certain measures and targets (believing them to be indicative rather than mandatory) or inclined to take a literal interpretation of 'what they have been told to do', attempting (unrealistically) to comply with every measure and priority. In certain cultures they might also be ill-equipped – due to ingrained attitudes towards non-confrontational styles of managerial behaviour – to conduct mandatory performance appraisals where the non-achievement of certain outputs can be discussed openly for improvement purposes.

How do effective AMs manage outputs to the satisfaction of 'controllers'? The first thing that needs to be said is that, given the plethora of measures that apply in most MUEs, AMs can never meet every output criteria set by their superiors or organisation (except in exceptional circumstances such a uniformly underperforming district or unit for which they have just taken responsibility). More realistically, successful AMs conduct a *gap analysis* and target their most serious output variances.

HOW AMS ANALYSE AND CLOSE THE GAP (GAPPAR)

- **Gather**: Assemble all key organisational performance objectives
- **Analyse**: Conduct GAP analysis of portfolio/unit performance against objectives
- **Prioritise**: Identify the 'big rocks' that will accelerate performance (20/80 'wins') and break down into unit/section-level sub-goals (write them down!)
- **Plan**: Formulate and implement plans: by whom, by when? ENSURE METRICS AND KPIs ARE 'MICRO' TRANSLATED/ CASCADED TO COLLEAGUE/TEAM MEMBER LEVEL (see case study below)
- **Advertise**: Tell others about the plan and benefits (including peers, support staff and superiors); it is thus more likely to become a self-fulfilling prophecy
- **Review**: Measure performance outcomes; incrementally improve

As AMs are measured on district-wide metrics, making a significant difference in a small number of serially defective stores can have a disproportionate impact on their overall numbers. To this extent, AMs are portfolio optimisers, concentrating upon raising **relative *and* absolute** metric performance through targeted rather than wholesale interventions. This requires high levels of cognitive/interpretative nous, courage and managerial skill. The difficult task confronted by the AM is to locate the *causal factors* which have led to underperformance. For sure, AMs might know what the output issues are; but what are their input dependencies?

HOW TO MAKE P&L INPUT/OUTPUT LINKAGES

Output Issues	*Input Fixes*
Declining £ Sales	service (speed, knowledge & politeness), pricing, standards, range, product quality, promotions/ events, marketing, merchandising, availability, skills and capability (staff turnover/stability) etc.

Declining £ Margins	cost of goods, price elasticity, sales mix, shrinkage, wastage, stock/inventory levels etc.
High Labour Costs	sales ratio, deployment/rostering efficiency, multi-skill capability, shift leadership effectiveness, productivity/ discretionary effort, process effectiveness etc.
High OMCs	consumables (over stocking), energy (plant, operator error/procedural non-conformance), main- tenance (lack of checking/supervision) etc.

Any number of input fixes might be required to resolve output issues. It is the role of the AM to locate patterns that can rectify the P&L. Making *conscious* linkages by focussing on the obvious dependencies will undoubtedly yield some success for AMs but it is also important that they have the capacity to use their *unconscious mind* to deal with issues and solutions. This involves knowing what needs to be decided/solved and distracting the conscious mind in order to allow the *unconscious mind* to work away to solve/make sense of complexity.

One major area in which AMs are constantly called upon to make adjust-ments/interventions – given the proportionately high cost to MUEs – is the labour line ratio (i.e. cost of labour as a percentage of sales). Fixing labour costs when they have run out of control is a major bugbear of AMs: what are the common issues and – outside of normal organisational interven-tions (such as weekly hours/cash targets) – what can AMs do?

HOW DO AMS FIX THE LABOUR LINE?

Common Issues	Solutions
Volume/Capacity Mismatches	a) **Accurate demand forecasting**: last year/current year 'run rate'/upcoming events/weather/monthly 'payday' calendar
	b) **Capacity design**: manning levels, key role 'fills' (shift leaders, hosts, production, service etc.), accounting for holidays/absence/maternity
	c) **Unit-level labour 'lead'**: responsibility desig- nated to experienced personnel with 'micro-market' knowledge
Unit Responsiveness	a) **GM accountability**: i.e. link bonuses to t/o and labour spend (e.g. wage bill multiplied by 4.5 to set the t/o target – t/o 'over target' results in 15% bonus split amongst colleagues),
	b) **On-site flexibility**: contracts (seasonal 'flex'), core/peripheral (full time vs part time), annualised

	hours, late-notice 'shift swap/reduction' facilities
Productivity & Discretionary Effort ('do more with less')	**a) Work/job design**: designated roles and responsibilities, multi-skilling
	b) Deployment: rostering ('right complement, right people, right jobs, right time!'), linking staffing to volume and capacity, accounting
	c) Process simplicity: simplifying the service delivery system through removing unnecessary process stages ('touch points') and/or solving pinchpoints through investment in technology, facilities and/or machinery 'enablers'
	d) Store/shift leadership: 'in session' motivation of high performers, REMOVAL OF POOR PERFORMERS
	e) Extrinsic motivators: rewards and incentives (session/day/week/month/quarter/annual)
	f) Intrinsic motivators: selection, development, avenues for progression, empowerment (complaint resolution), resources to do the job, honouring promised hours/holidays

As has previously been stated, AMs are confronted by a myriad of output measures and controls; but which ones are really important, to whom and why? What are the real boundaries and tolerances, i.e. which breaches really attract sanctions and/or punishment? Effective AMs create and sustain *'insight networks'* that can help them locate truth, meaning and knowledge within the organisation. These networks can operate horizontally amongst their peer group or upwards amongst the strategic population of the firm. Such relationships help AMs understand, beyond formal narratives of what constitutes acceptable behaviour and conformance, what the implied or informal rules, procedures or codes of the organisation actually are. It is only through creating a wide network that the AM can collate and process information that generates understanding as to what constitutes an effective platform for action. To this end, the means by which effective AMs activate and sustain an 'insight' social network to help them prioritise outputs are as follows:

HOW DO AMS CREATE 'INSIGHT NETWORKS'

- Locate senior managers/peers that have high 'truth' value
- Create peer relationships based on exchange
  - swapping hard and soft resources

- Build organisational networks through mechanisms such as:
  - participating in working parties
  - volunteering for trials and best-practice initiatives
- Understand 'organisational reality' of controls and objectives
- Interpret information and formulate plan of action based on insights

The data and information gained from social networks, when added to the formal objectives, goals and measures of the organisation, can act as an additional filter for prioritising goals within the portfolio.

Case Study 9: Data Linkages and Action Prioritisation in YO! Sushi, Browns, All Bar One and the Premium Country Dining Group

Vanessa Hall is the Chief Operating Officer of YO! Sushi. Previously, as Brand Operations Director, she ran a collection of premium businesses including Browns, All Bar One and the Premium Country Dining Group.

… Whilst the guys at the top of the organisation will (usually) be numerate and have a high degree of financial understanding, this is not necessarily replicated down the organisation… nor is there ever an effective training focus on this area! … Linking inputs to outputs is not especially well done by many operators. In my experience, however, when I think of the best AMs, they tend to have one thing in common: they can immediately 'read the P&L' and interpret the relationships between sales and profit conversion AND understand what the intervening causal factors might be. In my view, this is a skill that really does 'take you further' in organisations. But what do the best AMs do? In my experience they do three things:

- *Data analysis*: Truly effective AMs will leverage both monthly and weekly data for insights:
  - Monthly: This is generally historical data when AMs receive it (often six weeks old) but does provide the 'pieces of the jigsaw'.

CONTINUED …

- Outputs: The best AMs will be able to pull apart the P&L outputs pretty quickly – unpacking, in particular, what I term 'gearing'; that is, the ratios of costs (such as labour, COGs and wastage) against sales. Where sales are 6% up and net profit is only up 1%, there are clearly 'gearing' issues – but what are they and, more pertinently, what is causing these problems and how can they be resolved?

- Inputs: Further information on issues/opportunities will be located by the effective AM in other sources such as empathica (customer data), team stability/engagement figures and compliance reports. Data that trends against the best performing units will provide clues with regards to customer advocacy/propensity to return, staff morale/discretionary effort and systems/standards adherence – all factors that will affect both sales and 'gearing'.

- Daily/weekly: AMs will receive daily data on sales and labour costs: weekly data on stocks. Again, this is a mine of information on trends and likely 'gearing' outcomes at the end of the month although it is more about the 'what' than the 'why'… In addition, effective AMs will be capable of accurate sales forecasting – something that inevitably facilitates better gearing outcomes and continuous improvement…

- *Prioritisation*: Having gathered the data and made a desktop interpretation of what is going on effective AMs will 'hit the lows'. That is to say – having had a monthly review with their retail director (where they will discuss how they focus their best people/time on the biggest opportunities which are not necessarily the 'low contributing underperforming businesses) they will go to the units within their portfolio with the biggest opportunities on sales/'gearing' issues and sit down with the GM and/or the KM to discuss solutions. The questions they will usually seek to address are:

- How can we stimulate value-added sales?

- How can we (sensibly) improve the gearing, further increasing sales-to-profit conversion?

- What short-/medium-term actions do we need to take in terms of process, productivity and capability in order to produce results?

CONTINUED …

Very often, in my experience, one of the major issues will be FOH/ BOH interfaces. Either the GM is insufficiently trained in food production processes (particularly in premium environments) and so has no 'grip' on labour, quality, processes, stocks, wastage and compliance in the kitchen; or in some cases, the GM and KM just don't get on, leading to a lack of communication on targets and objectives. Given the high costs of food production in premium food-service units, the GM–KM relationship is absolutely key to performance; if costs run out of control in the kitchen, 'gearing' goes up the spout!

- *Local translation*: What I have found is that some GMs and KMs don't understand simple concepts such as % gross margin profit... At a roadshow once, I could see some GMs shifting in their seats with embarrassment when asked a simple question on the subject! ... So what the best AMs do is, first, improve the degree of GM/KM financial literacy and interpretation skills and, second, help them break down the super-ordinate targets of financial plans/review into understandable bite-sized chunks. This is what I call 'articulating' – breaking corporate/area/unit objectives into relevant day-to-day targets. Often policy makers are too far away from the units and the P&L language they use is at best convoluted – at worst downright gobbledegook! Great AMs are translators, articulators, motivators – they make the complex simple for both FOH and BOH operations... making sure objectives are broken down for communication in pre-shift meetings... For instance, if desert wastage is a problem and 'fresh' product such as cheesecake is the main issue – incentivise staff to upsell it so that write-offs can be eradicated! Also, effective AMs will teach business planning skills to their GMs – anchoring objectives and targets to what most great businesses do – *increase sales whilst controlling costs*!

THREE KEY 'PRIORITISATION AND LINKAGES' QUESTIONS FOR AMS

1. Do you understand the key interdependencies of your P&L (the 'input' factors which drive each 'output' metric) AND regularly complete gap analyses at both district and unit levels? (If not, use the GAPPAR checklist above!)

2. Have you articulated 'macro' KPIs at a 'micro' level in your district? (That is to say, you must make sure that 'super-ordinate' KPIs are broken down at service-provider level to drive behaviours!)

3. Are you managing the labour line (your biggest controllable cost, your most important 'customer asset'!) with savagery or sophistication? (See above for tips!)

VALUES AND INTENTIONAL BEHAVIOURS

Alongside blueprint monitoring and output prioritisation – practices which might be termed *bureaucratic controls* – MUEs often develop a type of socio-ideological narrative exemplified through a 'values system' (either tacit or codified – expressed through company websites, induction programmes, CEO missives, etc.) which is the code of required behaviours that are the basis for practical and ethical action. These are intended to shape attitudes and guide purposeful/intentional behaviours that provide the moral standards for 'permissible' conduct within the organisational clan. In some instances – most pertinently within international contexts – these act as a corrective against ingrained personal or cultural values which might subvert the way (according to what the organisation wishes) in which people are treated or day-to-day business is transacted. Given that personal values are derived from three principal phases – birth (0–7 years), imprint (8–13) and socialisation (13–21) – organisations have much work to do in some cultures in order to overturn or countermand received truths. To this extent, organisational values require *bounded* and *purposive* statements of 'the way we do things around here' in order to ensure that, in the absence of explicit instructions, members – rather than falling back on pre-programmed defective behaviours – are acquainted with what is the 'right thing to do' in most circumstances.

VALUES SYSTEM PURPOSE

- **Cultural control**: Form of soft control system for the organisational 'clan' (e.g. IKEA: 'togetherness', 'down to earth' and 'hardworking')
- **Purposive statements**: 'Way we do business around here'
- **Intentional behaviours**: Leads to assured outcomes for the organisation in the absence of explicit commands

The broad reality is, however, that while organisational values are intentional ideological mechanisms that seek assured behavioural outcomes they will often come up against a number of barriers:

VALUE SYSTEM BARRIERS

- **Country base values**: Might undermine/not be aligned to company values
- **Mixed messages**: Contra behaviours by senior leaders
- **Personal values**: Due to prior imprint and socialisation, some employees do not 'fit' with company values

The question therefore remains as to how organisations develop and encourage AMs to ensure adherence to their codes of conduct/values and how AMs encourage their team members to do so as well (especially in emerging/developing market contexts)?

HOW DO MUES AND AMS INCULCATE VALUES?

- **Testing**: Many MUEs actively test the 'value set' of applicants to establish their level of fit.
- **Immersion**: 'Socialisation' through intensive training and consistent communication from senior leadership
- **Intolerance of breaches**: Immediate sanctions for misconduct or failure to apply the 'right' behaviours
- **Standard bearers**: AMs will make a conscious effort to act as standard bearers and exemplars for their organisation's values even when they run counter to extant local cultural norms, for instance basing appointments and/or rewards on performance rather than relationships.
- **Cultural value changes**: As some emerging economies experience economic enfranchisement (leading to higher levels of education and greater exposure to developed norms – such as emancipation and democratic institutions – through travel/digital media) some of the values espoused by international organisations become a better 'fit' for those espoused by transitioning societies.

Case Study 10: Values Transmission in Burberry

Reg Sindall was EVP Group Resources (encompassing four customer- and three employee-facing functions) for Burberry Plc (350 units globally).

… In my view, successful MUEs now take what I term a *multi-layered* approach to attracting local talent… *First* – and most importantly – recruitment systems should be aligned the firm's *core values* (which in the case of Burberry were 'protect, explore, inspire') which by turn are anchored in the company's purpose (made all the more powerful if it has a strong emotional connection). What does this mean? It requires local recruiters [HR, regional, area, store managers etc.] first, to have high levels of self-awareness as to what is required to function effectively within the ambient organisational culture and then, second, locate and calibrate appropriate talent that voluntarily *buys into* and *fits* (through attitude, behaviour and disposition) these espoused *values*… sometimes these *values* might transcend local ones… but getting local colleagues to believe in and commit to the *why and how?* is essential… Upholding and reinforcing these values through constant messaging, communication and modelled behaviours is also key… at Burberry we had transitioned our CEO quarterly webcasts down to monthly ones accompanied by real-time, company-wide Facebook interaction… *Second*, MUEs need to pay attention to extrinsic 'glue' mechanisms (although emotional buy-in always precedes this)… at Burberry every employee was placed in a performance incentive scheme and were shareholders. Third, extensive training and development systems are required to show that the company is prepared to invest in skills that benefit not only the organisation, but also employees' portability and sense of worth.

With regard to service training, simplicity and consistency of approach [i.e. *values alignment*] are the most important factors… The service delivery system at Burberry was called the 'Burberry Experience' with which all employees were made conversant, what-ever their level, position, function or location… [I]nterestingly, this programme… which was easily understandable and digestible…

CONTINUED …

had been developed through empirical analysis of the [values and] behaviours of the best sales associates globally and then packaged as a consistent approach to drive *intentional, passionate* and *purposeful* behaviours… In addition [this programme was] underpinned by constant endorsement through senior management making frequent international store visits, regular regional conferences and awards ceremonies, where store, call centre and HQ-level service excellence (i.e. politeness, knowledge and quality) was publically recognised and rewarded! … [S]uch events also provided excellent networking opportunities across our international operations…

THREE KEY 'VALUES AND INTENTIONAL BEHAVIOURS' QUESTIONS FOR AMS

1. Understanding that your people cannot 'take a manual onto the floor', are you sufficiently confident that not only will they 'do it right' but *also* 'do the right thing' in most circumstances?
2. Is the 'right way to act' clearly defined and understood at district and unit level?
3. Is it aligned to the organisational and/or your own value sets?

DELEGATION AND NETWORKS

A key attribute of effective AMs is their ability to reduce physical distance by improving their span of control through *delegating* important objectives, tasks and functions to individual team members. Alongside this, the process and content of delegation is enhanced by the degree to which the AM leverages 'insight' and 'enabling' *networks* within the organisation. Taking delegation first, effective AMs are archetypal distributed leaders. Given time and physical/spatial constraints allied to the scope and breadth of their role, they succeed by successfully distributing ownership of key tasks and objectives, leveraging the human capital that they have at their disposal. Delegation, however, involves trust and the ability to 'let go', something that many AMs newly promoted into the role from unit manager find notoriously difficult. As previously stated, at first unit managers tend to try and run their district as a series of independent units, in effect trying to manage and control each specific store as they had themselves done in the past. This leads to high levels of overload and stress and can be a principal reason why some AMs fail in their transition from unit to district level.

The types of delegation that AMs deploy will vary according to the capability, motivation and personalities of their followers, but broadly they will fit into six categories:

TYPES OF DELEGATION

- **Formal**: Intentional devolvement of activities
- **Pragmatic**: Activities devolved through negotiation
- **Strategic**: Specific skills/capabilities fitted with activities
- **Incremental**: Delegation is spread as experience increases
- **Opportunistic**: Activities distributed in an ad hoc manner
- **Cultural**: Delegation is naturally assumed organically and willingly.

It must be stressed, however, that the AM remains accountable for the performance outcomes. Delegation cannot be used as a means of shifting problems or abandoning culpability. To this extent, strategic and cultural, rather than pragmatic or ad hoc, forms of distributed delegation are likely to be far more successful within MUEs. The benefits of strategic and cultural delegation lie in the fact that, first, as the process empowers a degree of independent decision making, it can have a positive motivational effect on individuals who are granted a degree of influence that they might hitherto been lacking. Second, delegation can have associated payoffs such as saving time, money and bolstering capability within the portfolio. Done badly, however, delegation can have negative consequences such as stress and frustration on the part of the individual deputed to execute the specific activities and confusion amongst the wider team. In terms of process, delegation is likely to be most effective for AMs when it is done in the following manner:

DELEGATION BEST PRACTICE

- **Clarity**: Clear tasks/responsibilities/objectives
- **Impact**: Subordinates can influence outcomes

- **Agreement**: Understanding, acceptance, buy-in
- **'Fit'**: Development and/or skills fit
- **Support**: Resources, training and emotional
- **Communication**: Update wider team on progress
- **Review/recognition**: Regular monitoring and contribution acknowledgement.

But what architectural form does delegation usually take within portfolios? Depending on MUE context and AM preference, formal/informal delegative structures that help to 'spread the load' for AMs – also reducing the *'bystander effect'* in their wider teams (where people can 'hide' and dodge responsibilities) – usually take the following forms:

HOW AMS STRUCTURE DELEGATION

- **By Geography**
  - **Cluster/family lead**: Responsible for optimising hard/soft resources in a group of sites that are in close proximity
  - **City/town lead**: Co-ordinating role (with regards to pricing, promotions etc.) in single or multi-brand/format entities to prevent cannibalisation.
  - **'Hub and spoke'**: Large 'hub' store acts as the main 'geographical anchor' with regards to training and stock 'run downs'.

- **By Process**
  - **Process lead/expert**: Nominated person within the portfolio is assigned responsibility (due to their skills or expertise) to be the 'point man' (monitor, improver, upgrade handler, district representative) for:
    - Process area: Labour, talent management, stocks, hygiene and safety, customer service, administration etc.
    - Projects and initiatives: Centrally driven change programmes, district improvement projects etc.
  - **Houses of excellence**: Due to levels of operational excellence certain sites are used as exemplars and 'teaching houses' where portfolio members are taught or new initiatives are trialled.

Case Study 11: Cluster and Process Delegation

Mark Henderson (MSc LLS with distinction 2014) is the area manager for 12 Mecca Bingo Clubs in Scotland.

… In the past, the performance of the Scottish business has lagged behind those based in England… but the past year we have turned it around – a major contributor (I believe) being the geographical clustering of groups of clubs… hence clubs around Glasgow and those in north-east Scotland have held localised cluster meetings where they address common issues in the local market… things like promotional scheduling, combatting competitive threats and meeting distinctive local consumer needs… [A]t times central and even area objectives can seem somewhat disconnected to the requirements of local markets (in terms of ticketing pricing, promotions and F&B)… [W]hat we have done is shifted analysis, insight and informed decision making closer – in demographic and physical terms – to the customer (without compromising the brand)… something that I believe has paid dividends in performance terms as we have given greater control and autonomy to those closest to the fire! …

Andrea Strathmore (MSc MULS with distinction 2014) is the area manager for a multi-brand portfolio of twenty units for Stonegate, a major pub restaurant company.

… I work for an extremely professional outfit that has liberated the culture of the business from its previous ownership regime… one thing that I have been permitted to do is cluster my units on a geographical basis – even though they are spread amongst a multi-brand format/segment (young venue, locals, classics and traditional) – to ensure that they don't conflict locally and work together to optimise sales… For instance, a unit that has early breakfast openings can market the 3 a.m. late licence of a neighbouring outlet – and vice versa – with both units gaining through reciprocation… my three or four pub clusters can also work on differentiating themselves locally by talking through what each other's businesses do during the week and what seasonal events they are planning… what

CONTINUED …

the rhythm of their businesses are... This environment also allows close trust-based relationships to flourish enabling knowledge sharing and high degrees of 'soft' and 'hard' resource sharing... but overall I would say that devolving some kind of autonomy to tight geographical clusters has released a powerful force of discretionary effort and 'can do' attitude due to GMs thinking that they can shape their environment/destiny...

David Stallard (PGDip MULS with distinction 2014) is an area manager (16 units) for Hungry Horse (200+ sites), one of the UKs fastest growing mid-market family pub restaurant chains.

... After I took over my current area eighteen months ago, I carved my district into three physical clusters, all led by HIPO GMs... this would enable me to spread the management load and delegate certain functions... [W]hat I found, however, was that whilst these operators were excellent at executing standards and systems in their own houses, they were not necessarily well-equipped for multi-site tasking in terms of auditing and/or business planning... [I]ndeed, these clusters now fulfil more of a geographical 'point of reference' function where GMs come together to share ideas and knowledge... What I have concentrated upon instead is creating a cadre of *process champions* who can cut right across my portfolio; my first appointment being a GM who is my 'right-hand man' *kitchen champion*... this individual – an expert in his own right – will devote one day a week, outside of his unit, helping to drive standards, compliance adherence, ergonomic flows and food-quality systems by providing coaching, training and advice... So what I have opted for is expert process capability that cuts across the portfolio rather than *just* clusters; probably a better idea in a 'harder brand' environment where blueprint execution, rather than localised customisation, is the key driver to success! ...

In addition to practical delegation within their portfolios, effective AMs locate and leverage *'enabling networks'* throughout the MUE. In practical terms this involves identifying key people who can help them in their day-to-day execution of the role such as administrators in key support functions – supply chain, payroll, recruitment, training, maintenance and marketing/promotions, for example. As their role often involves smoothing out operational problems and troubleshooting on behalf of their units, effective AMs identify the key contacts (who are not commonly direct reports) that can help resolve specific blockages or friction points. As they are competing for scarce internal resource, effective AMs are expert in creating bonds and relationships whereby they derive at least the same or greater level of *internal service* than their counterparts. Given problems of space and distance, this is a time-consuming activity but one which is ultimately highly beneficial in terms of net outcomes. In general, the means by which successful MULs go about creating and leveraging a valuable 'enabling' social network are as follows:

HOW AMS CREATE 'ENABLING NETWORKS'

- Identify key operational support staff enablers
- Create relationships based on exchange: friendship, financial or goal fulfilment
- Understand formal and informal rules of engagement
- Leverage support for portfolio
- Sustain relationships through continued exchange.

Case Study 12: Mobilising Internal Support Services for Meet & Eat

Mike O'Connor (MSc MULS with distinction 2014) was jointly responsible for operationalising the Meet & Eat franchise concept in a major pub restaurant company, which has subsequently become a 'lead' brand (120 sites) within its estate of 900 managed units.

Having been chosen as one of the two area managers to set up and roll-out a new franchise concept in our estate called Meet & Eat (a 'hard' brand initiative which would, first, give certainty/consistency to the value-led customers using our unbranded community assets and, second, provide a viable vehicle for prospective franchisees), I had to mobilise support functions within the organisation to provide us with essential services… The barriers one inevitably faced were

CONTINUED …

those relating to functional detachment... our concept would not be their only agenda, so we had to make sure that we deployed a number of strategies to garner critical support services... [W]e did this through a number of ways:

- *Power/authority*: By telling support personnel that this initiative had strong support from the senior leadership team, we were able to co-opt services by emphasising the strategic imperative of the project. But this only worked with a select number of people, given that people don't react well to veiled threats and there was no guarantee that what we were doing would be successful!

- *Recognition*: In the case of some functions we identified individuals who were willing to help and publicly recognised/praised their support. For instance, one of the EPOS data processors in IT became a really good contact – she was highly responsive to our requests to change pricing on the tills, in response to franchisee requests (say discount pricing on soft drinks for certain periods)... she understood the importance of responding quickly to franchisee requests – given the commercial business relationship and service-level requirements... [W]e encouraged and rewarded her behaviour by always recognising a 'job well done' through office visits etc. ... [H]er 'little' task had a big impact on the way we were perceived by our franchisees...

- *Education*: With some functions we spent a great deal of time educating internal service suppliers through explaining the concept and our needs. For instance, food purchasing needed to slightly adapt the way they communicated out coding changes on menu items for the franchisee community... By sitting down with key managers and administrators, we were able to get them to buy into what we wanted and they then adopted a totally different communication approach.

- *Relationships*: In some instances, we had to use high levels of social capital to improve internal processes that impacted upon franchisee perception and morale. For instance, in administration we were highly fortunate that one of our ex-colleagues in the line had been seconded into the centre and we were able to utilise his empathetic support to ensure that food recharging processes, royalties and marketing fees were properly administered in addition to standard processes...

So co-opting and mobilising internal support services is really about carrot and stick… but the approach that will always win out (lending willing and sustainable back-up) is the carrot approach, where you invest time and patience to find/build willing allies!

THREE KEY 'DELEGATION AND NETWORKS' QUESTIONS FOR AMS

1. Have you delegated responsibilities within your district to appropriate 'SKILL OR WILL' personnel either by geography or process (or both)? (This is absolutely essential – DELEGATE OR PERISH!)

2. Do you regularly monitor, review and (where necessary) recognise their contributions?

3. Do you use the talents and services of 'enabling functions' in the wider organisation – delegating tasks and responsibilities where possible? (Again, creating/fostering friends in support functions is crucial for SURVIVAL/SUCCESS!)

AUTONOMY AND DEVIANCE

The word 'autonomy' is derived from an ancient Greek word meaning 'living under one's own laws'; in organisational terms, it is related to sanctioning space for individuals to make un-coerced choices and decisions – typically expressed as 'freedom within a framework' or 'empowerment'. It is regarded as desirable because a degree of self-determination is believed to increase control by virtue of the fact it generates (in exchange terms) increased effort, motivation and commitment, ensuring that staff take a flexible approach to problem solving – useful given that not all MUE rules and procedures fit every situation. *Less control can paradoxically lead to the organisation's ability to exert more order and outcome certainty.*

The principal issue with autonomy is that of where it should start and end. Unlicensed autonomy in the absence of rules and values can lead to anarchy and disorganisation, the very antithesis of what organisations are designed to achieve – order, control and dependability. Some MUEs will allow local decision making and/or micro-market customisation with regard to store-specific promotions and/or local buying. In some 'soft' brands, up to 30% of the product ranges of stores can be determined locally in response to competitor activity and/or in response to idiosyncratic local needs. Other 'corridors of autonomy' open to exploitation by AMs include aspects of unit-level roles and responsibilities. Effective AMs will encourage unit managers to show imagination and ingenuity around certain processes such as selection, training, service, local community interaction and such like. For instance, establishing links with worthwhile local charities and encouraging teams to think of ingenious ways to raise money will not only serve to embed businesses in their local communities but will also serve the dual purpose of creating a feeling of independence, identity and worth within the unit team. The pay-off from this is that, by granting a degree of latitude and independent decision making, the AM is, in effect, exchanging a degree of freedom in return for control and compliance in other areas. Best practice tips as to how AMs are able to grant/ leverage autonomy are therefore as follows:

HOW DO AMS GRANT AUTONOMY?

- Understand MUE's 'freedom within a framework' rules and norms
- Identify viable 'corridors of autonomy' that will add to rather than subtract from business performance
- Ensure staff have the appropriate skills and mindsets to cope with 'freedom within a frame'
- Sanction autonomous behaviours in exchange for conformance in other areas
- Review impact and effects of independence

The techniques referred to above can act as a transactional exchange device to ensure more general conformance. The common denominator is that they are generally sanctioned by the organisation at large and fall within the formal boundaries of permitted behaviour. Research shows, however, that on occasions effective MULs will consent or turn a blind eye to breaches of company standards, rules and procedures if they believe that either the 'law is an ass' or that there are better ways of doing things. This behaviour can be termed 'added value deviance' (AVD) because, whilst such behaviour might be deemed illegal by the organisation, it might actually serve to improve the performance of operations and, again, act as an exchange for compliant behaviour in other regards. Sometimes within MUEs, the line is well ahead of technocrats in the centre in terms of what the customer expects and what might give them competitive advantage within local micro-markets; thus senior operational personnel will conspire to give tacit approval to breaches that add manifest value. This is generally well-received by front-line operators and will generally assist – as a form of tacit exchange – in helping the AM to assert control in other areas ('if I let you do *x* then I demand *y*!'):

HOW DO AMS REGULATE AVD?

- Check that staff have appropriate skills and mindsets
- Ensure prospective rule breaking is added value *not* value destructive (i.e. don't 'blow up the machine')
- Enfold the process with trust, removing fear of retribution (i.e. inform 'friendly' higher authorities)
- Ensure all participants are bound by a sense of morality and ethical behaviour
- Review and check outcomes

Case Study 13: Social Media AVD in Food Service Co

Susie Palmer is an area manager for 16 branded value food-service units in Food Service Co (FSC) (pseudonym), a large UK-based hospitality corporation. Previously she was a general manager of several value-led branded restaurants. This is an extract from her Leadership and Change essay on the PGDip Multi-Unit Leadership at BCU in 2014.

… The scorecard meetings also prove to be a hotbed of innovative solutions. There is an obvious risk in creating this environment of innovation in a large organisation. FSC is a risk-averse company that has historically sought to centralise efforts rather than allow localised activity. Whilst this is a culture that is changing gradually, there are still occasions when local opportunities to grow sales and guest advocacy are refused due to a perceived risk. My role in this environment is therefore to make the correct choices around value-added deviance. In a recent scorecard meeting, a manager delivered a presentation to the management team which highlighted

CONTINUED …

the opportunity that social media afforded us on a local scale to drive awareness of offers in our businesses. Given the pressure that the brand menu trial had placed on our average spend per head, I understood the need for localised marketing to drive footfall and reach new guests. The proposition raised was regarding marketing boosts on business Facebook pages which – for a fraction of the national marketing cost – could drive significant local guest awareness of the daily offers available. In this case, for £12 a manager had added 4,000 additional followers to his business's Facebook page by tactically advertising existing offers. This was received well and adopted by the management team as a great way to interact with our guests locally and drive awareness.

This represented such a significant potential sales opportunity that I shared this with my colleagues at our meeting later that month. However, the marketing team felt that this fell outside social-media policy guidelines and that as such it should not be acted upon. In this circumstance, I agreed with the GM! ... [T]he opportunity was too great to miss and was being used by our competitors locally; in my view, the risk was greater if we failed to take advantage of this opportunity. I put some process around this and ensured that I had one lead manager accountable for regularly checking the content of these pages, but otherwise acted on *trust*. My managers wanted to do the right things for the right reasons and I was happy to support them in this within a protected environment.

Value-added deviance should, however, not be confused with questionable ethics. I believe the consistency of my actions is the bedrock of generating trust and engaging my team. I work on the basis of informed trust. If the correct behaviours are evident but the outputs are poor then I believe this to be a capability issue and offer support and retraining. I am not an advocate of constant performance management through disciplinaries, as I believe it to be an unnecessary time drain and completely counterproductive to the building of relationships. In my view, it is far more productive to focus upon training and coaching performance in the vast majority of cases. However, if trust is broken, I act swiftly and will hold the individual to account. The amount of trust provided is directly related to the capability of the manager, thereby mitigating unforeseen service performance issues...

THREE KEY 'DEVIANCE AND AUTONOMY' QUESTIONS FOR AMS

1. Are you aware which elements of the brand are fixed and which are flexible?
2. Have you alerted your GMs to areas for self-expression/ autonomy?
3. Where you have permitted 'deviant' behaviour outside prescribed rules, is it fully legal and does it add value to the business?!

SUMMARY

The previous chapter referred to the multiple commitment-based interventions that effective AMs apply to *reduce distance* between central policy-makers, themselves, their followers and customers. This theme was continued in this chapter which considered the means by which effective AMs deployed a number of bureaucratic and values-based control practices to close down distance. From a *structural* perspective, geographical forms of *delegation* (clusters, families, and hub and spoke) utilised the power of self-managed teams, relieving some of the onerous and burdensome tasks from AMs. Also, 'bureaucratic processes' of *monitoring, enforcement and prioritisation* enabled AMs to close down *hierarchical* distance between the centre and the units. *Networking* and *blueprint monitoring* had the effect of reducing *functional* (i.e. outsider and vocational) distance, whilst with regard to *psychological* distance, AMs freed up capacity through an ideological form of control – judicious application of a *value system* that encouraged *intentional and purposive behaviours*. Hence, as the AM cannot be present at every site at once and many decisions at unit level cannot be checked off 'against the manual', the effective AM modelled and prescribed a set of values that informed and guided positive behaviours. *Psychological* distance was further strengthened by the effective AM allowing some degree of local autonomy and AVD with regard to product, promotions and people.

Ultimately, it is the ability of effective AMs to 'let go' (once they have locked down the operational essentials) that marks them out as ultimately more successful than their peers – not least because this gives them the capacity to do other things such as continuous process improvement, innovation and knowledge diffusion across the portfolio – as the next chapter will illustrate.

CHANGE

The third dimension of the professional practice of effective area management, alongside the intertwined activities of generating commitment and exerting control, is implementing change. Disruptive forces faced by the MUE have accelerated the nature and pace of change in many firms and sectors over the past few years. As Chapter 2 highlighted, policy makers have had to react to the challenges wrought by economic instability, technological innovation and altered consumer behaviour by attempting to adjust many facets of their business model and value chain to new environmental paradigms. These policy makers, by turn, have been reliant on the operational line to enact and implement transformational changes, with AMs – positioned between the centre and the units – being charged with efficient and effective execution of a plethora of centrally driven initiatives at unit level. To a certain extent, the calamitous economic environment of 2007–2012 in 'developed' economies provided a 'burning platform', creating organisational climates that were receptive and conducive to change, assisting the role of the AM in this process.

However, as the organisational behaviour literature relating to change elucidates, the function of creating, implementing and sustaining both transformational and incremental forms of change is a complex process that requires a highly sophisticated and sensitive approach. This chapter will, firstly, outline some academic commentaries relating to change and then consider the dynamics between MUEs, AMs and change. Second, given the flexibility that some business models afford units in terms of micro-market customisation due to idiosyncratic buildings and local markets (i.e. site, size, layout, labour, demographics, competition etc.), consideration will be given to how AMs promulgate both top-down and bottom-up improvements through: *adjusting mindsets and benefit upselling, leads and champions, patch ups and workarounds, continuous process improvement* and *knowledge diffusion*.

UNDERSTANDING CHANGE

ACADEMIC COMMENTARY

The academic literature conceives of change as a constant feature of organisational life, generally triggered by external forces. Its general narrative views macro pressures such as the economic environment, globalisation, regulatory intervention, commodity scarcity, unremitting technological development, changing composition of the external labour market and consumer expectations for quality and affordability as increasing the pace at which organisations have had to evolve their product in order to maintain efficiency and competitiveness. In response to these challenges, many organisations have had to embark on organisational change programmes promulgated by existing or, more likely, new leadership, with numerous goals including behavioural modification, increased organisational flexibility, enhanced people capability and the introduction of new technology or work practices (Chang and Harrington 2000).

However, the process of conceiving and implementing change is ridden with problems, not least the levels of resistance and inertia to change at both an organisational and individual level:

- **Organisational resistance**: In the literature relating to change, one of the main themes is the degree to which the middle of the organisation represents a real barrier to change (Reis and Pena 2001). Given technology-enabled changes to patterns of organisation over the past thirty years, with delayering initiatives reducing the numbers of middle managers (the survivors being expected to fulfil more tasks and duties), the role of today's middle manager is acknowledged as having increased in complexity, effort and workload (Mintzberg 2009). Added to which, many middle managers have, through e-business enablers, been relocated out of offices into 'working from home environments', and so the psychological burden of work, without supportive social structures, has become, for some, intolerably stressful. To this cohort, change has become a byword for extra work, eliciting a high degree of dissatisfaction, scepticism and resistance. Managers are apt to behave reactively rather than proactively to change because of the negative consequences for their work–life balance and perceived threats to their security and status.

  At an organisational level, cultural barriers such as embedded norms, values and accepted ways of behaviour also act as blockages. Organisations have generally grown through being successful in addressing markets in specific ways in the past. The strategy, structure and processes of the organisation, supported by belief in the 'way in which we do things around here', have been sufficient for success in the past, and therefore act as formidable barriers to change. There are also vested interests in maintaining stability: people have insufficient skills and capabilities to do what is required in the new world. Where their power, status or influence is likely to be undermined or threatened by change, they are apt to fall back on previous structure and contract in order to protect their position. A natural consequence of this level of countervailing force to change is that policy makers are often left with little choice other than 'change the people' in order to enact their change agenda.

- **Individual resistance**: Although organisations exhort workers to embrace change, there are strong psychological reasons why people resist:
  - Disorientation: First, there is the dimension of 'future shock' where 'among many (managers) there is an uneasy mood – a suspicion that change is out of control' (Toffler 1970: 27). Wave after wave of change couched in positivistic managerialist rhetoric is juxtaposed against its reality of disruption and chaos for many people in the middle and lower tiers of the organisation.

  - Lack of benefit: Most individuals, rather than embracing change, are fearful of its disruption to their identity and well-being. Change upsets routine and habit, often leading to restrictions on freedom and autonomy. Individuals are often attached psychologically to the past 'when things were better' and experience a sense of disorientating loss in a future state that they find hard to believe will bring improvement and progress. From a transactional perspective there is also the fear that destabilisation will bring costs such as reduced financial incentives and increased sanctions.

So how do organisations create a state of readiness for change? Lewin's (1951) classic text relating to planned organisational change and behaviour modification advocates that managers can only facilitate successful change if they transition people through three stages:

- **Unfreeze**: First, the organisation needs to be *unfrozen*; the forces that maintain behaviours in their current form should be reduced before any progress can expect to be made. This might involve extensive communication and development to increase 'change readiness' or, in extremis, removing impediments through whole-sale people changes.

- **Movement**: Second, the organisation needs to be *moved* to where – in conjunction with new attitudes and behaviours – new policies, structures and norms are introduced to the organisation.
- **Refreeze**: Third, changes in behaviour and policies need to be *refrozen* and reinforced through the new supporting practices and structures.

Critics of this approach cite the difficulties that managers have in transitioning organisations in such a deterministic and prescribed manner given attitude, time and resource constraints. Also, such an approach infers that change is a planned 'big event' rather than an ad hoc, organic, incremental process – as it usually is, especially in multi-unit enterprises (Volberda et al. 2001). For sure, the notion is compelling that one of the principal functions of managers is to facilitate preparedness for change. A major issue, however, relates to the fact that many managers lack the necessary skills to manage change (Crainer 1998) and that many remain behind the curve in terms of mindset and disposition (Drucker 1989). Crainer identifies seven skills that managers require for managing change including:

- Ability to manage conflict
- Strong interpersonal skills
- Project management capability
- High levels of leadership and flexibility
- Capacity to manage processes
- Ability to manage 'self' and one's own development
- A mindset that moves beyond managing the change curve (i.e. change leaders should seek to 'be ahead' of the game not only anticipating and embracing change but also actively engaged in framing change policies of the future).

In terms of transformational change, one of the most influential contributions to effecting high performance change within organisations is provided by Kotter and Cohen (2002). In their eight-step model of change implementation, they bring together many of the elements required for lasting transformational change:

- **Create a sense of urgency**: Inculcate process with a sense of pace and dynamism

- **Build a guiding team**: Ensure actors have skills, credibility and organisational connections
- **Create visions**: Sensible, clear and uplifting representation of the 'to be state'
- **Communicate**: Widely broadcast the goals and strategy to induce commitment
- **Empower action**: Remove obstacle that impinge achievement
- **Produce short-term wins**: Provide the process with credibility, attracting further resources and momentum
- **Don't let up**: Consolidate early changes and create 'wave after wave' of changes
- **Make change stick**: Nurture a new culture and embed group norms of behaviour and shared values.

Again, their approach can be criticised for its determinism and also a presupposition that policy makers, first, have the capability to apply such an approach and, second, actually know what they are doing. However, its concept of pace and short-term wins to galvanise the organisation have merit in organisations where levels of inertia and resistance are high.

With regards to incremental change – excepting techniques such as TQM, Kaizen, EFQM and self-managed teams – a useful contribution is made by Hamel (2000):

- **Establish a point of view**: Create a credible, coherent, compelling and commercial POV based on hard data.
- **Write a manifesto**: Infect others with your ideas. Capture their imagination with a picture of how you can resolve their discomfort.
- **Create a coalition**: Assemble a group of colleagues who share your vision and passion. Present yourselves as a coordinated group speaking in a coordinated voice.
- **Pick your targets**: Go after the suits. Find some that are searching for new ideas and, if necessary, bend your ideals a bit to fit their goals.
- **Co-opt and neutralise**: Disarm and co-opt adversaries rather than humiliating and demeaning them. Reciprocity wins converts; ranting leaves you isolated and powerless.
- **Find a translator**: Find someone who can build a bridge between you and the people in power. Senior staffers and newly

appointed executives are often good translator candidates – they're usually hungry for an agenda they can call their own.

- **Win small, win early, win often**: Demonstrate your ideas actually work. Start small. As your record of wins grows longer, you'll find it easier to make the transition from an isolated initiative to an integral part of the business.

MUES, AMS AND CHANGE

Reference has already been made to specific issues confronting AMs, not least their control of widely dispersed sites and their precarious situation, positioned between the centre and units. The section above covering the academic commentary on change provides some understanding of the way in which change occurs within organisations and the mechanisms that managers may deploy to execute it successfully, both from a transformational and incremental point of view. But what are the specific idiosyncrasies of change within multi-unit enterprises and how do effective MULs institute performance-enhancing change?

During the course of my previous research, a consistent picture emerged relating to the nature and characteristics of change within MUEs. These can be grouped around five main insights:

- **'Crippling initiativitis'**: Most multi-unit organisations suffered from what one respondent called 'crippling initiativitis' where wave after wave of ad hoc, uncoordinated initiatives 'rained down' upon the units.

- **Central bias**: Most change initiatives were generated from the top with little involvement from those down the organisation expected to implement the changes.

- **Third-party reliance**: With large transformational programmes, organisations seemed to lack the self-confidence to do it themselves, preferring to place their faith in third-party change consultants who were co-opted by the centre to redesign processes or structures.

- **'Hard' initiatives rule**: Given the economic environment and the focus of many organisations upon cost, most change initiatives focused on 'hard' rather than 'soft' operational drivers. Hence new technology applications designed to improve labour productivity, stock control and shrinkage were more common improvement initiatives than those focussing on customer service.

- **'Soft' initiatives drowned out**: Soft interventions focusing on people and service largely died or were postponed in order to accommodate the focus on cost-saving changes.

It is within this broad context that AMs are expected to enact change. The literature cited above referred to the necessity for organisations to explain, communicate and involve people in change in order to ensure its success and sustainability. Yet my research consistently found that many multi-unit enterprises failed to adhere to any of the best-practice principles advocated by experts in this area. The economic 'burning platform' argument was used as a universal justification for many changes, although staff remained sceptical as to whether 'cutting costs to victory', rather than a sales- and product-led approach, constituted a long-term, sustainable strategy. Nevertheless, some AMs were able to function effectively within this adverse context, producing exceptional performance results in the midst of this challenging environment. How did they enact change and what techniques did they deploy in order to survive in such adverse circumstances? Previous chapters detailing how effective AMs generate commitment and exert control have emphasised the significance of exercising social exchange in order to optimise the portfolio. Whilst this remains true with regards to implementing effective change within the portfolio – especially in terms of *adjusting mindsets and upselling benefits* and nominating *leads and champions* – there are also practical interventions that AMs can make to facilitate change. Effective AMs engage in identifying successful *patch ups and workarounds* to ameliorate badly conceived initiatives from the centre but also stimulate *continuous process improvement* and *knowledge diffusion* throughout both the portfolio and the wider organisation. These practices will be considered in turn.

MINDSETS AND BENEFIT UPSELLING

Change is an unremitting feature of MUEs with organisations having constantly to review, adapt and modify their business models to ensure that they maintain competitive efficiency and effectiveness. However, the *process* of implementing change is dependent on creating an environment in which recipients are in a state of 'readiness' with mindsets that are adjusted to embrace rather than resist. If the definition of 'mindset' is a *cognitive bias* – a set of established assumptions held by individuals or groups that inform behaviours and choices, and can create mental inertia through 'groupthink' – organisations have a major task in ensuring that their people maintain a high degree of open-mindedness and flexibility in order to absorb and enact vital initiatives. But how does the AM assess the change readiness of his followers?

HOW DO AMS ASSESS CHANGE READINESS?

- Age, education, capability, behaviours
- Morale and psychological preparedness
- Previous experience of change
- Location of resistance and counterforces:
  - active and passive resistors
  - lack of time and capacity

When enacting organisational change, AMs potentially face several problems. First, from an operational standpoint, changes to work systems, tasks and process flows that were deemed appropriate at policy-making level are not applicable/implementable locally unless levels of resource, capability and expertise are sufficiently factored into programmes. Second, MUEs must always take account of the fact that, in the past, the benefits of change have been overstated in comparison to personal costs (job security, time, effort, disruption etc.). So how do AMs of international MUEs adjust mindsets amongst their people to accept change as an imperative?

HOW DO AMS CHANGE MINDSETS?

- Review and address own mindset and self-esteem
- Reset follower mindsets:
  - stasis is not an option; constant 'refreshment and change' message
  - focus members on controllables
  - reinforce sense of contribution and importance
  - address wilful saboteurs and blockers
  - create capacity through task allocation (see 'Leads and Champions' below)
  - sanction patch ups and workarounds (see 'Patch Ups and Workarounds' below)

In addition to addressing self and team mindset – setting the foundations for change management – the effective AM judges every change initiative in terms of cost-benefit analysis. That is to say, effective AMs actively seek to understand and communicate the benefits of change, weighing up the extent to which these benefits act as a positive exchange for the implied or real costs for their people. For instance, some inventory process changes might be complex to understand and operate at first – due to new electronic procedures – but in time they reduce overall workload by automating what had previously been done through form filling or over the telephone. Hence benefit upselling has a major part to play in changing attitudes and behaviours.

HOW DO AMS UPSELL BENEFITS?

- Make a cost-benefit analysis of change (Benefits – Costs = Outcomes)
- Avoid 'overblown' benefits statements – 'polishing the turd'
- Present realistic summation of benefits (e.g. efficiency) and personal costs (e.g. time and effort)
- Provide time and space to 'learn' and 'unlearn'

It is important to emphasise that, during the selling of new changes, benefits should not be oversold and costs (time and effort) should be realistically expressed. At times, the AM will have to counter rather overblown benefits statements from the centre concerning the virtues of some new initiatives, responding to their assertions with more 'grounded' reasons as to why a change might be beneficial. Also, given that the centre tends to underplay costs, the degree of realism that the effective MUL brings to play in this area can only add to his/her credibility and degree of authority within the team. But learning how to overcome objections at *every stage* of the change process is a necessary function provided by the AM.

HOW DO AMS OVERCOME OBJECTIONS? (AMOAA)

- A – Acknowledge/empathise
- M – Make specific
- O – Overcome/answer
- A – Assess reaction (hot/cold)
- A – Agree action (close!)

Case Study 14: Adjusting Mindsets and Benefit Upselling in Mecca Bingo

Mark Henderson (MSc LLS with distinction 2014) is the area manager for 12 Mecca Bingo clubs (circa 100 nationally) in Scotland.

... In line with our vision of 'Thrill the Nation', Ian Burke (CEO of Rank Plc) and Kevin Allcock (Operations Director) challenged our central teams with the task of devising and organising a 'show-time' event that would 'wow' our customers. This event came to be known as Firecracker, where customers – paying more than they usually would do – would be enticed to a one-off event at one of our venues which would mix big party entertainment and high-level atmospherics alongside large cash prizes. To date we have had 11 Firecracker events around the country, all becoming progressively more successful and impactful. I was brought on board by the CEO to manage this project and make it happen following initial deliberations by the project group. However, selling the concept into all stakeholders was not easy. Who were these stakeholders, what barriers did they present and how did I overcome them? I'll go through each stakeholder in turn:

- **The centre**: One of the first barriers to progress I faced was a degree of inertia from some central functions. Why? The simple fact was that – perhaps due to a lack of operational/customer 'closeness' at head office – people saw the downsides before recognising the upsides. In order to get buy-in, I presented to the Mecca Executive where most of the HODs attended and sold the potential benefits of Firecracker: the fact that it aligned with our vision and would increase advocacy – excite existing customers and potentially attract lapsed members and 'non-users' etc. I also talked to the HODs on a one-to-one basis outside of the meeting to get their support... I have to say that in the end they really rallied around. As the project unfolded, I also briefed them on the changes we were making to improve the offer to make sure they maintained confidence in what we were doing.
- **The clubs**: At club level there was resistance from GMs who – I believe – were more frightened about failure: would the IT

CONTINUED ...

systems crash on the night? Were we capable of managing such a huge event with 1,000+ customers 'paying top dollar' with high expectations?! How would they cope with ticketing, queuing, F&B delivery, new technology, stage management etc.? In order to allay fears, what I did was: first, present to the GMs in areas where a club had been nominated for Firecracker and talked to GMs individually; and second, put together a team of local GMs where events were being held with complementary skills. One was an expert on FOH service, another F&B, another gaming and theatrical presenting etc. Therefore Firecracker became a joint project in areas, where the nominated site did not feel isolated and other clubs felt more involved. Areas now felt 'this is our Firecracker'!

- **The customer**: There were a couple of teething problems at the first event but, after this and a couple more, we listened and considerably improved the product. We actually increased the price of the ticket from £50 to £60, allowing us to provide our customers with a shot of winning ten pots of £10,000 on the night – life-changing amounts of cash. Also, we ramped up the atmospherics/entertainment and improved F&B delivery on the back of their feedback. Its success with customers was such that many of those who attended one of the original events in one of my clubs in Glasgow travelled all the way to Blackpool for one of the next Firecrackers!

Over the duration of this project we have certainly improved the product and got our competitors talking about it – when I was in Foxwoods last week (one of the largest gaming centres in the US) even they knew about it! In order to sustain its success we will keep talking and listening to all stakeholders to ensure it maintains its momentum!

THREE KEY 'MINDSETS AND BENEFITS' QUESTIONS FOR AMS

1. Are YOU mentally attuned to the necessity/inevitability of policy, technology and product/service changes?

2. Are you sufficiently equipped (in terms of both mindset and information) to overcome resistance/objections?

3. Can you increase follower readiness to accept/implement changes by upselling their benefits (increased sales/efficiencies)?

LEADS AND CHAMPIONS

In relation to helping team members to 'unlearn' past behaviours and practices and adopt new ones, effective AMs do two things: they master the change brief themselves and co-opt process leads/champions within the portfolio to 'train out' the changes. The previous chapter (in the section 'Delegation and Networks') considered how effective AMs delegate specific control functions with defined responsibilities and feedback mechanisms; the process of transmitting change is similar, albeit there will be a defined start and finish point to the process. The important point is that, given the breadth and complexity of their roles, AMs cannot possibly succeed in implementing change unless, first, *they* understand its detail and nuances and, second, they get their people to do so as well.

In terms of the former aspect – mastery of the detail in order to establish credibility – effective AMs will acquaint themselves not only with the reasons *why*, as outlined above, but also the *what* and *how*. They will ask a number of questions and (in certain circumstances) equip themselves with the wherewithal to train out the changes themselves.

HOW DO AMS UNDERSTAND CHANGE INITIATIVES?

- Five key questions:
  - Aim: What is this change designed to do?
  - Effect: What impact will it have on operations?
  - Difference: How is it different from what has gone before?
  - Content: How does it work?
  - Process: What is the timetable for implementation?
- Familiarisation:
  - Training and immersion
  - Train the trainer

With regard to co-opting champions, smart AMs – who have already delegated certain key functions within the portfolio to nominated team members – will identify overlap, assigning additional change responsibilities to the same individuals, ensuring optimal alignment and expertise. Thus, the nominated team member responsible for labour productivity systems will also be assigned responsibility for understanding and 'training out' upgrades or major changes. In major one-off change projects that are either too large or that fail to overlap with existing delegate responsibilities, effective MULs will co-opt a number of 'cluster change champions' who they will utilise in ensuring that knowledge and skills are transferred as quickly as possible. Clusters within the portfolio will generally be identified on a geographic basis, allowing nominated champions to train out efficiently in units that are based nearby.

HOW DO AMS CO-OPT CHANGE LEADS?

- Understand the minutiae of the change
- Identify overlaps with current delegated responsibilities within the portfolio
- Create capacity for nominated personnel (i.e. temporarily backfill to cover absence)
- 'Train out' to process experts or nominated 'cluster champions'
- Change leads drive adoption and roll-out
- Monitor and Review

Case Study 15 – Designated 'Leads' at Sainsbury's

Simon Jones is the Regional Operations Manager for 21 units with Sainsbury's (150,000 colleagues and over 1,000 stores).

… One of the most important things I learnt on becoming a ROM was not to try to manage every unit directly but to lead my GMs to manage their stores even better. But, given the amount of change going on within the organisation, what I also had to do was distribute responsibility across the portfolio. Why did I do this? First, I could

CONTINUED ...

not possibly oversee every change initiative directly because of time and expertise constraints. Second, I wanted to drive accountability down to store level and improve the capability of my store managers.

The way I have achieved what I call 'diffusion' is to take the scorecard and ask my team who would like to 'lead' or become 'portfolio holders' on a specific element. This led to managers coming forward to 'lead' on availability, mystery customer, talent development, cost control, labour productivity etc. It was important that they put their hands up – it might have fitted their skills area or, in some cases, provided the opportunity for further development. What these 'leads' then did is send out briefs and e-mails to their colleagues on developments, changes and initiatives in the areas that they oversaw. They also provided capability workshops in their stores to educate other store managers and their teams on the 'what, how and why' of their specialism. At regional meetings they also had the opportunity to request agenda time to brief out changes in their area and/or train initiatives on. The question remains – how do I monitor and keep control of this complex web?

Since an element of their annual assessment is made around 'personal contribution' levels, I can keep a check on the degree to which my 'leads' have discharged their duties effectively – particularly with regards to keeping up-to-date with changes. This 'personal contribution' assessment is linked to incentives so there is quite a high motivational factor here where my store managers will be actively demonstrating to me that they have effectively led the areas for which they are responsible. Take my 'Talent Lead': there is a lot of change within the portfolio with new systems and vacancies – what this 'lead' did was put together a really good talent matrix and development programme, based on his intimate knowledge of the area and work with the HR Business Partner, which has kept abreast of change in the region. In recognition of the work he had done, I gave him 100% pay out due to his 'personal contribution'.

The way I chase progress is through personal development reviews or ad hoc discussions through my 'visits with a purpose'. Where are we with the implementation of such-and-such change? What

CONTINUED ...

are the blockages? What can I do to help? Most large companies are averse to change, so what I find myself doing is acting as an intermediary and facilitator for my leads to help them drive things through – getting them the resources (manpower and cash) to make things happen. Is this approach successful? In my experience, it follows the 'third, third, third' principle... The top one-third are brilliant – they have bought in totally and see the benefit of their position... they can make a difference... it also puts them on the radar if their contribution is noted elsewhere (which I make sure of!)... This means that for the really high-profile areas within the company or the area's most susceptible to change, if you the right attitude and skills you can really get things done...

THREE KEY 'LEADS AND CHAMPIONS' QUESTIONS FOR AMS

1. Have you got delegated process experts (i.e. for talent, service, labour costs, range/stocks, compliance, promotions/marketing, new openings etc.) in place to interpret/co-ordinate central initiatives?
2. Although responsibility is delegated, you retain accountability! Are you sufficiently up to speed with implementation progress?
3. Do you back your leads/champions in public forums, recognising their contribution through praise/recognition?

PATCH UPS AND WORKAROUNDS

Reference has previously been made to the fact that, given the distance of the centre from the units, its failure to use (or listen to) operator expertise in the conception of new change initiatives, coupled with its lack of insight into the minutiae of unit operations (due to few operators transitioning into jobs 'in the centre'), many change initiatives in multi-unit enterprises might be ill-conceived or badly thought out. The AM now has a choice: does he accept the change initiative lock, stock and barrel or seek to make (legal) alterations that make the initiatives more workable? For sure, many AMs, fearing sanctions from the centre for non-compliance, will adopt the former route, passively accepting what they 'have been told to do'. However, braver, more self-confident AMs (a state usually born from experience) will not accept the status quo, either suggesting modifications to the centre immediately to enhance chances of the initiative's success or making adaptations themselves following consultation with their teams. In this sense, they are acting in the same manner that was referred to in the previous chapter: sanctioning added-value deviant behaviour for high-performance purposes. The main difference in this instance is that within the context of change they are, as one respondent put it, 'permanently on watch actively to divert sewage from the centre!'

In the first instance, effective AMs will try to make modifications by sanctioning 'patching up' the deficiencies of the change initiative. This means that, having understood the detail of the change initiative and consulted with their nominated champions or team, (s)he will sanction improvements that will add value to the efficiency and effectiveness of the initiative.

HOW DO AMS 'PATCH UP' DEFECTIVE CHANGE?

- Sanction adjustments for 'fit' purposes:
  - process: with limited 'bandwidth'/capacity, increase timescales
  - content: allow legal alterations (e.g. pricing policies in merchanting)
- Gain permission from higher authorities

In exceptional circumstances, effective AMs will 'work around' certain initiatives because of their poor conception/design. This is not to say that they fully reject the objectives underpinning the initiative: 'workarounds' fulfil the main intentions or *ends* of the initiative without any resort to the *means* suggested by the policy designers. This is a highly dangerous strategy that, in the hands of inexperienced or over-exited operators, can foster and embed bad behaviour. Living solely by the dictum that 'the ends justify the means' can lead to chaos and anarchy in standardised multi-unit contexts. Nonetheless, there are instances where, after mature and rational consideration, implementing a 'workaround' strategy can pay dividends.

HOW DO AMS IMPLEMENT WORKAROUNDS?

- Adjudicate on the efficacy of the change (where possible)
- Investigate how 'ends' can be met without resort to content or process 'means'
- Effect change in a different manner to increase efficiency/impact
- Seek permission to avoid sanctions/penalties

Case Study 16: Standardisation versus Customisation in Jewellery Chains

Paul Clowes was Group Display Executive for Signet (550 units; H. Samuel and Ernest Jones) and currently advises multi-site jewellery firms on display strategies. Previously a multi-site manager, Paul has 35 years jewellery multi-site experience.

… The role of the field in enhancing/adapting central change and/or initiatives is dependent on three factors: *capital spend*, *seasonality* and *brand positioning*…

With regard to *capital spend*, the field will have ample opportunity during new store or refit designs to make inputs into FOH and 'off sales space' (i.e. BOH storage, administration and delivery areas) configuration based on local knowledge… Regional managers, familiar with the site location and dimensions, will advise the Store Development Team (SDT) and Visual Merchandising Team (VMT) on the best entrance positions, store flows, storage dimensions (based on turnover) and product adjacencies etc. … eventually signing off the agreed projects…

In respect of *seasonality* – autumn/winter and spring/summer collections – store segmentation having already been pre-determined centrally in terms of category grades (i.e. categories such as diamonds being split into solitaire, cluster, eternity and coloured sub-components) merchandising/product packs will be sent out automatically to stores… The best AMs drive the 're-set' benefit of

CONTINUED …

seasonal range changes immediately; slower operators (claiming lack of staff hours etc.) that are tardy suffer as a result... However, regional/area managers have some latitude on range and can request extra brands (particularly watches) outside of the normal cycle... They are also involved in a constant cycle of meeting with the buyers (say at regional meetings) where they can provide feedback on what is going well/why and what display components might enhance the range...

But where the greatest opportunity for local adaptation occurs lies in relation to *brand positioning*... Volume/value brands such as H.Samuel imposed rigorous planograms with pre-set display pads and fixed pricing; giving field managers little opportunity to innovate beyond the prescribed format... However, in a premium/variety brand like Ernest Jones the field was given more latitude through magnetised 'free dress step-up' displays which local operators could (within reason) configure according to local micro-market demands... Other multi-site jewellery operators I have advised grant more autonomy on product selection, pricing and display at a local level... here the AMs and store managers are encouraged to 'read' the local market and adapt product and display to 'fit'...

The question therefore arises of what is best – 100% standardisation or customisation?... The answer is probably neither; although fixing perhaps 70% of the offer and allowing 30% 'localised autonomy' might be preferable, dependent on the culture of the brand, its positioning and the capability of its people...

THREE KEY 'PATCH UP AND WORKAROUND' QUESTIONS FOR AMS

1. Are central initiatives generally 'fit' for local purpose?
2. If not, can you or your team *customise* the initiatives for maxim local impact?
3. In extreme circumstances (having had permission from above), can you ignore unworkable initiatives because your current ways of working are better/more resilient?

CONTINUOUS PROCESS IMPROVEMENT

Whilst effecting the head office's demands for transformational change programmes and/or top-down initiatives is important, AMs must also lead and encourage the practice of continuous process improvement at portfolio and unit level. In most MUEs, every site is different. Due to footprint constraints (imposed by landlords and/or legacy real estate) and locational differentials that impinge upon the rhythm of the business (i.e. demographic profile, high street versus mall etc.), the AM has ample opportunity to make improvements to the FOH process flows within each site. In addition, rather than accepting BOH standards and procedures as a 'fait accompli', HMUL and their teams have ample opportunity to make *value-added* adaptations that fit with the operational needs of the business.

What AMs should seek to do, when assessing improvements, is examine a process (which can be defined as the movement of 'transformed inputs' consisting of customers, information or materials from one stage to another) and assess whether or not they can make improvements to its speed, cost, dependability, flexibility, quality or safety. Can they eliminate non-value-added activity stages, time-wasting decision points or blockages/pinchpoints? In normative terms, process effectiveness is derived from staff, technology, machinery and facilities (the 'transforming inputs') being applied and aligned efficiently to processing aforementioned 'transformed inputs' (Slack et al. 2009). Productivity gains arise when the effort and expense of the 'transforming inputs' are reduced whilst producing a greater volume and quality of outputs. Clearly, at outlet level, great advances in efficiencies can be made by organisations that instigate (piloted and proof-tested) process improvements. However, the capacity of individual units (assisted by HMULs and their peers) to make significant differences in operational capability should not be underestimated.

IMPROVING PROCESSES

- **Definition**: 'The movement of materials, customers, information from one stage to another where added value activities occur'
- **Objectives**: Low cost, high sales, speed, dependability, flexibility, safety and quality
- **Shapers**: Staff, technology, facilities and machinery

- **Desired outcomes**: Throughputs/rhythm: Removing pinch-points and barriers and/or improving machinery/technology/staff capability will increase throughputs 'rhythm of the business'
- Dependability: Reducing the number of process stages and decision points increases dependability and limits operator error
- Capacity utilisation: Good processes maximise capacity through rapid customer 'turn' (i.e. customer order fulfilment)
- Input reduction (i.e. staff costs/effort) and output optimisation (i.e. sales and productivity)

As most AMs have been unit managers, the first thing that needs to be said is that they have probably been promoted (amongst other reasons) for their ingenuity and proactivity. That is to say, many AMs in MUEs have already proved that they possess a site-level aptitude for initiating micro-process improvements. They will also have a high degree of *curiosity*, having garnered a number of insights from a variety of sources such as competitor site visits and observations from other units within the MUE. Now they need to lead by example by, first, making an assessment of the process efficiency of their units and, second, cheerleading and rewarding best-practice behaviour. As to the former, AMs will become acquainted with their individual sites and, whilst doing so, will ask themselves the following questions:

HOW DO AMS ASSESS AREAS FOR IMPROVEMENT?

- **Location**: How good is this location? How visible is it? What is its footfall? How can we attract more attention?
- **Car parking**: What is the car-parking capacity? How safe and secure is it? Is it used solely by our customers?
- **Layout**: What is the size and layout of the unit? What are the FOH and BOH blockages?
- **Service cycle**: What is the customer journey from entry to exit? How smooth is the experience? What are the *functional* blockages?
- **Experience**: What senses are stimulated positively by the visit? How effective are the *emotional* stimulants?
- **Product and promotion**: Does the range address the local market? Are the promotional mechanics fit for purpose?

So when and how do AMs actually improve processes? Along with their units, AMs will have a degree of human, physical and financial resource (or 'sleeve'!) which they can judiciously deploy (sometimes nefariously) in order to make significant improvements. During a refit, the AM and his team have a major opportunity to make the store more efficient and attractive (both for themselves and customers) if they work closely with the refit team (i.e. project managers, building managers, architects, store improvement leads etc.). By and large, however – given that sparkles or refits rarely occur within a four-year cycle in most MUEs – the AM is required to rely upon extant resources and latent ingenuity to promulgate process improvements. Effective AMs are also more likely to stimulate unsolicited, spontaneous behaviour not through setting an example by doing it themselves but by rewarding and recognising exemplar improvement behaviours at all levels in their portfolio, fostering a culture of continuous process improvement. As failure is a required feature of improvement and innovation – and therefore might be rejected in cultural environments where rule adherence and obedience are obligatory – AMs might *transfer risk* from individuals to 'collaborative teams' where increased risk taking and experimentation is deemed 'safer'. How this knowledge is transmitted across the portfolio and wider organisation is also important and will be the next behaviourally based change practice to be discussed, in the section below.

HOW DO AMS IMPROVE PROCESSES?

- Analyse: Gather quantitative data on throughputs/capacity utilisation
- Observe: Watch operations 'in the field'; spot the 'rate limiters' (see above)
- Plan: Draw up 'resourced' plan of remedial action (i.e. funds for training, new machinery, facilities and/or technology enhancements)
- Do: Delegate plan of action with agreed milestones to nominated personnel
- Review/reward: Regularly monitor (sanction adjustments?) and recognise added value performance
- Embed: Incorporate improved process as a BAU (business as usual) activity

- Rollout/diffuse: If the process improvement has a generic application, rollout across the portfolio (see 'Knowledge Diffusion and Innovation' below)
- Isolate/tolerate failure: If process 'enhancements' fail, accept the cost – move on

Case Study 17: Evolving Harvester Restaurants

Steve Cash was the Brand Operations Director for Harvester Restaurants (210 units) and Miller & Carter (31 units), 2008–2013. In 2011, Harvester was the winner of the Peach Coffer Brand Evolution Icon Award.

… When I took over Harvester in 2008, it had just been featured on a programme called *Rogue Restaurants* where operational malpractice had been filmed secretly and aired on primetime TV. Frankly, the brand had lost its way after a few years of mismanagement: profit was spiralling and morale was at rock bottom. What I did first was get out into the estate – closer to the action – listening to and watching both customers and staff; working several shifts in the kitchens to get a handle on what was going on in the 'engine rooms' of the business. What I decided pretty quickly was that we needed to improve every aspect of what we were doing. This required an overhaul of processes/approaches with regards to product/menu, pricing, people, amenity/facilities and marketing to increase sales, margins, throughputs (covers) and capacity utilisation:

- *Product/menu*: Taking a guest perspective, it was obvious that our menus had become too confusing: 'a trip around the globe' I called it! For a brand that was essentially based around grilled chicken, ribs and a famous salad bar, we had added pizzas, curries and nine variously cooked fish dishes! When I tried to cook it off in the kitchens, I found I was using every cooking process known to man – a complete enemy to throughput and production rhythm! Also, storage of the ingredients was a problem… for slow-selling items (there were a lot of them!) you found that you were hunting through pantries, chillers and freezers to compile dishes. Also our bars were crammed with

CONTINUED …

beer fonts – presumably because marketing had agreed to supply deals in exchange for a few garden umbrellas! So what I did was streamline the menu and drinks range and get back to what had made it famous in the first place: grilled chicken, ribs and salad.

- *Pricing*: Prior to my arrival, there had been a misguided attempt to remove Earlybird (1/3 off the price for diners pre-6.30pm). This was a trademarked offer that had differentiated the brand since its conception over 30 years ago – the word itself representing value for money to guests; but it's time restrictions were causing operational crush! The problem lay not with Earlybird but with the rest of the offer. Because of the price disparity of pre- and post-Earlybird menu items, GMs were extending it beyond 6.30pm because they were doing little business afterwards – it had become their only throughput mechanism! What I did was put Earlybird on the main menu and close the price differentials (in some cases to £1) with some 'entry-level' dish options which gave customers the option to 'build' their dishes (with sauces, sides, add-ons etc.). We also stopped random price promotions – only changing our pricing at Xmas. Our pricing became honest, understandable and transparent. This meant that our customers began to trust us again! Because people came to dine with us post-6.30pm, we began to make more efficient use of our fixed assets.

- *People*: The brand had terrific people at team-member level and had high rates of stability. But due to the fact that the brand had grown its estate by a third after an acquisition of units from a competitor in 2005 (and then lost most of their people due to cultural issues), its AM, GM and KM population had become overstretched. Second-line management (in some cases) had become over-promoted. There was also an air of cynicism within the AM and GM population. I acted quickly to pull in really experienced AMs with high levels of food-production/service capability. They administered 'tough love', addressing GM capability issues fast – training, coaching and motivating. In the kitchens, we introduced an Accredited Chef programme, an extensive programme of NVQs and identified geographical Houses of Excellence. We also wrote directly to team members (at their home addresses)

CONTINUED ...

to explain the changes we were making, why we were making them and how important their individual part in it was.

- *Amenity/facilities*: We also invested in sharp 'sparkles' for our existing estate to address its 'tiredness'. Essentially, rather than spending £300k for a refurbishment, we injected £80k per unit in a targeted manner on F&F rather than just maintenance (we had just spent £1m on kitchen maintenance after the *Rogue Restaurants* programme). One particular project I instigated was called Project F, spending £20k per site to convert underused bar space into more covers. We kept the bars but put in dividers, utilising the 'freed-up' space (particularly window areas) to extend our cover capacity. Whilst our legacy customers continued to use their 'own' familiar space, our new customers were directed by hosts to these converted areas.

- *Brand extension*: Of course, no major change of direction could be undertaken without establishing how our current, lapsed and potential guest base viewed the brand. Thorough research was conducted and some of the feedback was brutal – be it warranted or otherwise! In essence, the brand identity had become lost amongst a large and homogenous mass of pub restaurants, which were also seen as dated and 'dirty'. It was clear that Harvester needed to explore new markets with new design… to be where societal eating-out habits had changed… to modernise and move into a new century, whilst retaining a 'one brand' agenda… Our move into retail and leisure parks was a huge step – a massive learning curve – but the right thing to do.

- *Marketing*: After a couple of years of smashing budget, confidence was riding high and the organisation started acquiring new sites. But as Harvester was predominantly southern-based, it lacked brand recognition in the north. We went back onto TV (in a positive way this time!) with an advert emphasising the brand's family friendliness, wholesomeness and warmth. Audited results showed that the campaign produced an immediate 6% increase in sales!

So what were the results? During the period 2008–2012 we increased average unit meal throughputs by 800 covers per week

CONTINUED …

(hitting 30m meals per annum). Other innovations/improvements we were working on included an extended breakfast offer, take-away facility, superior coffee product, better garden usage, digital marketing apps and food service technology. These will all continue to drive throughputs and capacity utilisation in the future!

THREE KEY 'CONTINUOUS IMPROVEMENT' QUESTIONS FOR AMS

1. Have you built up your capability to 'see the differences' in your operations and find areas of obvious process improvement that will yield value? (This is often derived from comparing your best unit with your worst!)

2. Are you sufficiently equipped to 'see the opportunities' in your units' local markets?

3. Have you and your team got the project-management skills to 'land'/seize the improvements/opportunities successfully?

KNOWLEDGE DIFFUSION AND INNOVATION

Given that most sites in MUEs have their own positional and operational idiosyncrasies, it stands to reason that there will be transferable insights which can add significant value both within the AM's portfolio and in the wider organisation. A major finding of my previous two books was that effective AMs acted as 'local leaders in multi-site operations' because, contrary to the view that standardised chain formats are optimally efficient if one hundred per cent of their operations are replicated throughout the whole estate, it was the author's observation that the most successful operations – whilst fixing certain immutable facets of their operation (usually BOH standard operating procedures) – tacitly adapted themselves to the peculiarities of their local micro-market. This could not be done solely on a top-down basis through head-office 'guessology', operating, as they might well be, hundreds or even thousands of miles from the theatre of operations.

Encouraging bottom-up tacit knowledge diffusion is hampered in most MUEs by a number of issues – not least due to distance but also by factors of their own making:

BARRIERS TO KNOWLEDGE TRANSFERENCE IN MUES

- **Lack of trust**: A belief amongst innovators that their ideas will be diluted/stopped
- **Different cultures/languages/frames of reference**: Inability to transfer ideas because of differing/resistant perceptions, attitudes and beliefs
- **Lack of time**: Distance and BAU activities prevent transmission/ adoption
- **Status/power**: Management layers and complex structures prevent transference
- **Limited recipient absorptive capacity**: MUE personnel do not have the capability (due to education, training and motivation) to absorb/understand ideas
- **Knowledge hoarding**: Possessors of innovative knowledge/ ideas guard it for reasons of 'internal competitive advantage' (due to the fact that MUEs set up their reporting systems to compare region against region, district against district, unit against unit etc.)
- **Error intolerance**: A belief of the generators of insights that if they fail to work in other contexts they will be blamed for mistakes.

Solutions to these barriers include: senior field visits and 'back to the floor' weeks; managerial rotation; and active feedback loops (i.e. daily/ weekly collection of insights by head office from front-line operators either by telephone conference calls or webinars). Also conferences, events, post-meeting meals and such like can encourage 'social capital' interfaces where deep tacit knowledge on how things *should* actually be done can be swapped in a trusting environment. Smart MUEs also have benefit-based reciprocity systems where 'sellers' of knowledge are compensated (through reward or recognition) if they transact with 'buyers':

SOLUTIONS TO KNOWLEDGE TRANSFER BLOCKAGES

- **Lack of trust**: Face-to-face communications (meetings, conferences, store visits etc.)
- **Different cultures/languages/frames of reference**: Education, team building, rotation of personnel (job rotation/placements/ short assignments/projects/working parties)
- **Lack of time**: Create time and space for idea swapping – deploy smarter methods for communication (digital solutions: webinars etc.)
- **Status/power**: Collapse hierarchies (remove unnecessary layers and get technocracy 'closer' to operators) – make ideas more important than status
- **Limited recipient absorptive capacity**: Educate employees for flexibility
- **Knowledge hoarding**: Reward/recognise the 'sellers' of knowledge and encourage reciprocity between parties through social capital
- **Error intolerance**: Remove gameplay, blame, sanctions and retribution.

But how do AMs encourage tacit knowledge diffusion (particularly with regards to reducing costs/increasing sales) across their portfolios? Many of the techniques referenced above will be used at portfolio level as well, albeit AMs will also adopt architectural solutions to sharing tangible and intangible resources by splitting their portfolios into geographical 'clusters', 'families' and/or a 'hub and spoke' format where tacit knowledge can be shared amongst small 'communities of practice'. In addition to this structural solution, AMs will apply relational interventions by leveraging district meetings, away days, training sessions and conferences to allow insights and knowledge to flow between parties formally. In practical terms, rotating unit managers or facilitating best-practice visits by unit managers (and sometimes their teams) to exemplar operations (whether owned by the company or by a competitor) are other means of ensuring knowledge acquisition. In addition, AMs will facilitate informal channels of knowledge transference which are particularly important because most research on knowledge transfer maintains that tacit (as opposed to explicit) knowledge is transmitted most effectively through means of social/relational capital.

HOW DO AMS ENABLE TACIT KNOWLEDGE TRANSFER?

- **Architecture** (reduce distance)
  - Geography: clusters, families, 'hub and spoke', stores of excellence
  - Process: leads, champions, 'experts'
- **Formal Channels** (facilitate 'PEER-TO-PEER'/'COMPETENCY-TO-COMPETENCY'-based learning)
  - District meetings and presentations
  - Placements/rotation
  - Teamworking (projects, initiatives, training sessions etc.)
  - Observation/site visits
  - Discussion forums
- **Informal Channels** (relational/social capital)
  - Social networks/discussion forums (i.e. Facebook)
  - Events, parties, celebrations (particularly after meetings, conferences, away days etc.)
- **Recognition**
  - Communication of 'wins'
  - Non-monetary rewards and treats

Where practicable, effective AMs will also engage, horizontally, with their peers and, vertically, with superiors and head office in order to garner valuable insights that they can transfer back into their portfolios/units.

Outside of encouraging tacit knowledge flows within MUEs, there is also a need to encourage formal innovation processes which will result in both invention and improvement (innovation = invention and improvement!). Whilst there is insufficient space here to discuss this in depth (for a practical example, see the case study below), there are many examples of formal processes advocated by MUEs which are used by AMs to stimulate value-added ideas at a portfolio level.

HOW DO AMS RUN A FORMAL INNOVATION PROCESS

- **Forum**: District meeting, away day or conference (but try and break the familiarity of surroundings!)

- **Buy-in**: Communicate the 'innovate or die'/benefits imperative (without overly increasing anxiety levels!)
- **Trends**: Examine local consumer trends, insights and developments
- **Gaps**: Surface gaps in current offer/systems/processes and potential opportunities
- **Brainstorm**: Value-added opportunities? (Allow group AND individuals time to surface ideas – groups are not necessarily the best vehicles for idea generation!)
- **Select**: Identify and prioritise 'big rock' runners
- **Test**: Pilot, measure, review and improve in store
- **Roll-out**: Implement (timetable and resource)
- **Recognise**: Reward and communicate

Things that must be born in mind by AMs, to ensure that any formal innovation process is successful include: eliminating '*social loafing*' and '*bystanding*' by group members during the process by spreading responsibilities and stimulating both the conscious *and* unconscious minds of team members (i.e. occupy conscious minds feverishly then do another activity to allow the unconscious to produce novel solutions/associations).

Case Study 18: Stimulating Innovation and Knowledge Transference in Stonegate

Andrea Strathmore (MSc MULS with distinction 2014) is the area manager for a multi-brand portfolio of twenty units for Stonegate, a major pub restaurant company.

… Stimulating innovation and knowledge transference throughout the units in my area is critical for a number of reasons. First, I want my GMs to be absolutely focused on sales growth for practical performance reasons. Second, I know that by focusing on the top line (whilst controlling costs) my GMs will feel that what they are doing is meaningful and worthwhile. Third, by getting excited about growing the business through new ideas, they are more likely to

CONTINUED …

swap insights and tips with their colleagues because, effectively, they are trading value-added information that could lead to reciprocation – benefiting them in the long run. Fourth, both the centre and I – because of our distance from the units and customers – do not have a monopoly on the best ideas; invariably the operators at the coal face know what the customers want and the things that will really drive sales! But how do I encourage innovation and knowledge sharing? Essentially, I stimulate it through the following 'multi-layered' approach:

- *Meetings*: I am quite clear with my GMs that what we have to do is 'get the basics' right first and then address how we grow the business. I do this in two forums:
  - Conference calls: Every Monday I host a conference call in which we look back on the past week's figures (in fact I have just come off one today!). What I do here is go through the numbers and make sure I provide a context to each remark, praising good performance and commenting upon positive trends – highlighting some of the things that my GMs have been doing.
  - District meetings: What I tend to do here is deal with the compliance stuff up front, ensuring we are 'safe' and have high standards. I will then let the GMs split off into their brands to discuss seasonal marketing plans or brand-based initiatives; sometimes we might hold these back-to-back in open forum for knowledge purposes. The latter part of the agenda, however, is completely taken up by the GMs (or in their absence, AMs or team leaders) presenting their monthly sales plans in five-minute presentation slots. This is where interaction, learning and swapping occur.
  - One-to-ones: I generally follow up these district meetings with one-to-ones regarding the practicalities of these sales plans: have the costs been thought through properly – are there any improvements that can yield further sales? Over the past few years, ideas that have yielded real improvements have been 'big ticket' items such as extended opening hours or licence variations, incremental things such as ad hoc events (fun days, quizzes, theme nights etc.) or mundane process improvements that reduce the cost structure of the unit.

CONTINUED ...

- *Clusters*: It is important, however, that the GMs get together on a local market basis – outside of large formal gatherings and meeting with me – to brainstorm how best to attack local markets. What they do here is talk one another through what each other's business actually does: its product/customer mix, rhythm of the week etc. Here tacit knowledge can be shared in a safe, informal environment.

- *Social events*: What I also encourage is good relations between my GMs through bonding at social events. Over the past year my district has won two incentives for 'seasonal drives' that *they* have allocated to spend on social events they want. These events create memories and stories – generating a sense of teamship that endures… [P]eople relax with one another – understand points of view… trust builds… resulting in valuable exchanges of insights and ideas.

Inevitably, the question is how you sustain this enthusiasm – particularly when your area boundary changes. What you do is keep working with the guys that really believe in improvement and innovation; let them showcase proudly what they are doing. The cynics, hoarders and doubters might eventually be won around by self-regulating behaviours within the group… [I]f they're not, they usually leave. Also, don't underestimate the enthusiasm of the unit teams and its power to make a difference. A team leader at one of my units came up with a security training poster that was taken up by my head office and rolled out across the company… [M]any is the time that ideas for events and new ways of doing things percolate up from team-member level!

THREE KEY 'KNOWLEDGE AND INNOVATION' QUESTIONS FOR AMS

1. Have you created a trusting culture in your district in which people freely swap information (on the basis of knowing that their peers will reciprocate!)? (The test of its effectiveness is whether it happens when you're not around!)

2. Do you allow appropriate time during meetings to allow cross-district learning to occur? (Don't forget the social side of meeting

up is just as important – bonds are formed and tacit information flows freely!)

3. Do you swap ideas and insights with your peers? (Don't hoard – give and you will receive!)

SUMMARY

The previous two chapters – 'Commitment' and 'Control' – highlighted how effective AMs deployed a form of professional practice that was aimed (either consciously or unconsciously) at *reducing distance* through the application of local leadership practices (local visioning, talent 'fit', service training and trust/recognition), 'operational grip' (monitoring, correction, prioritisation and values application) and the devolvement of responsibility (geographical/process-led delegation, autonomy and added-value deviance). These practices were recast in the summaries of each chapter to fit within the distance typologies previously elucidated by scholars who have examined variant forms of leader–member distance (such as Napier and Ferris 1993).

The change-based practices in this chapter can be similarly categorised. Hence, successful AMs reduce the *psychological* distance between the units and centre by *adjusting mindsets* and *upselling the benefits* of initiatives. In addition, they created *structural* capacity to expedite change through the deputation of initiatives to *leads and champions* within their portfolios which, by turn, frees them up to encourage *patch ups* and *workarounds* (ensuring that centrally conceived changes are properly melded to contextual exigencies). From a *functional* perspective, effective AMs reduced '*outsider*' effects through encouraging knowledge transference and the sharing of insights.

Indeed, in addition to the attributes of *energy, emotional intelligence* and *professional expertise* highlighted in the previous chapters, such mechanisms allowed them to exhibit a form of corporate *entrepreneurialism*. It is to these aforementioned personal characteristics of effective AMs that this book will now turn.

CHARACTERISTICS AND DEVELOPMENT

The previous chapters outlined the professional practices of AMs with regards to generating commitment, ensuring control and implementing change. Clearly the AM requires a number of job-related skills and competencies to expedite this role – but what are the characteristics of effective AMs? What attributes and associated behaviours are required for the effective discharge of this highly complex and ambiguous role? Through what means can these characteristics be developed? Addressing this subject is crucial for two related reasons. First, many MUEs use a generic set of competencies for selection and assessment of AMs which are derived from a wider population of the organisation (usually a middle-management band). This may neglect the nuances of the AM role. Such an approach does not guarantee any degree of outcome assurance for MUEs. Second, identifying high-performance technical, behavioural and cognitive characteristics pertinent to this role and their associated development interventions will assist MUEs in developing this vital cohort.

Based on my previous research, this chapter will outline five vital *characteristics* of effective AMs – expertise, emotional intelligence, entrepreneurship, energy and ethics – all of which have significant sub-components. After describing the various facets of each characteristic, the means of developing these attributes will be discussed. What will come through strongly to the reader is that *developing* AMs is problematic given the source of most appointees: unit-management level (UM). As has been previously stated, there are major differences between the job dimensions of these two roles, which, in caricature, can be summarised as follows:

Job Dimension	UM	AM
Span of Control	Tight	Loose
Management Approach	Direct	Indirect
Customer Intimacy	Close	Distant
Work Schedule	Defined	Fluid
Action Orientation	Do & Think	Think & Do
Primary Skills	Technical	Behavioural/Cognitive

Figure 7.1 Differences between UM and AM Roles

The implications of the difference in nature of the job dimensions of the two roles are significant not only for *what* those occupying the role need to know, but also for *how* they are taught and learn. UMs transitioning into the AM role are conditioned to absorb prescribed technical information through learning 'by rote'. As AMs – where far more complex thinking and problem solving are required – learning styles must be adapted to more of a 'critical reasoning' approach. The solving this conundrum will be explored below, in addition to consideration of the five main personal characteristics of effective AMs.

EXPERTISE

Expertise – the technical skills and knowledge applied in an impactful manner within the AM practice domain – is the first characteristic of the effective AM. From a general academic view there are two main approaches to understanding expertise: first, the *communities of practice* approach and, second, the *individual expert capacity* view. The former sees expertise as a socially constructed phenomenon where narratives and bias for action are shaped by groups, enabling members to codify, transfer and enact expertise within specific domains (Goldman 1999). Problems pointed out by this domain relate to the emergence of 'group-think' and isometric convergence that stifles original thinking (Janis 1972). The latter approach defines expertise as an innate characteristic of individuals which is formed as a result of absorptive capacity, environmental context and continuous and deliberate practice (Chase and Simon 1973, Ericsson 2000). Achieving expertise in certain fields or domains has been estimated by some commentators to involve 10,000 hours or a period of five years of complete immersion (Gladwell 2008). With specific reference to effective AMs, expertise manifests itself along three dimensions: *domain knowledge, professional practice* and *numeracy*, all of which lead to a high level of confidence and judgement.

DOMAIN KNOWLEDGE

Within organisations, knowledge manifests itself in both explicit and tacit forms (Nonaka and Takeuchi 1995). *Explicit knowledge* is expressed formally, being transferred through mechanisms such as written instruction and/or verbal communication. By contrast, *tacit knowledge* is difficult to transfer as it comprises informal habits and cultural idiosyncrasies which people and organisations are often unaware of possessing – just as they are also unaware of how it provides inimitable added value. Dissemination of this form of knowledge requires a high degree of trust-based personal contact and interaction.

The first characteristic of effective AMs is *explicit* domain knowledge of the sector, organisation and job. Thus, effective AMs will be successful in comparison to their peers through familiarisation and deep understanding of the following:

FACETS OF DOMAIN KNOWLEDGE

- Service-sector familiarity
  - Business-to-consumer transactions
- Organisational dynamics
  - Strategy/structure/culture
  - Supply chain
- Product/brand understanding
  - Positioning (value, mid or premium)
  - Functional/emotional drivers (people, promotion, place, pricing etc.)
- Blueprint mastery
  - Operational systems
    - labour processes, standard operating procedures, availability, stock & waste procedures, sales & pricing monitoring, due diligence and essential maintenance processes, ad hoc processes/change initiatives

- Brand standards
  - merchandising & display, internal environmental 'sensory' management, external environment
- Service delivery mechanisms
  - HRM, service concept adherence, customer feedback follow-up, service promise & complaints resolution.

COGNITIVE NUMERACY

Effective AMs will be successful in comparison to their peers in the achievement of many of their company-set objectives through domain knowledge; but it is not only their explicit knowledge of 'what matters' that counts. Rather, it is their *tacit* knowledge of 'how to do it' that separates them from the norm. In particular, effective AMs possess extensive practice-based knowledge, combined with superior *cognitive* thinking skills (highly connected to financial acuity), which enable them to unscramble how they can increase portfolio/unit performance – in spite of a wide span of control issues.

For instance, in the case of district and unit P&Ls, AMs are presented with voluminous amounts of information. How do they discriminate between the most significant data sets and indicators and, more importantly, focus upon what they need to do to improve performance? The answer is that they apply a high level of cognitive reasoning to a series of problematics arising from the P&L. Effective AMs are adept at locating patterns of dysfunctionality and/or opportunities to move the P&L in the right direction. These cognitive skills also apply to the prioritisation of measures, tasks and initiatives. However, although effective AMs involve their teams and local cluster champions in creating a local vision and prioritising/resolving certain challenges, the fact that accountability ultimately resides with them renders absolutely critical their ability to ensure that the *right things are being focused upon, at the right time, by the right people* through a complex process of association and reasoning.

FACETS OF NUMERACY/PROFESSIONAL PRACTICE
- 'Reading the P&L'
  - input/output dependencies/linkages
  - identification of causal connections

- Direction, prioritisation and delegation
  - local vision and clear direction
  - 80/20 prioritisation ('big rocks')
  - distributed delegation (leads, process champions, support staff 'enablers' etc.)
- 'Right person, right site, right time'
  - ensure appropriate GM–site fit

With regards to the latter point in the above, the process of ensuring the right GM–site fit is crucial in MUEs with the right unit manager being estimated to add 10% in sales in a retail environment and up to 30% in leisure. Thus, fitting the appropriate GM to a vacant unit with inimitable local market dynamics (from both a labour and customer point of view), one who melds with and *complements* the district team, is a non-trivial matter of professional judgement that is developed over a period of time.

DEVELOPING AM EXPERTISE

The development interventions that apply to new/existing AMs will vary according to prior experience, capability and situation. As a start point, AMs will obviously have to master the basics of the domain in which they are being expected to operate – something that newly appointed GMs (should) already possess. However, once the explicit factors relating to the role have been mastered, great attention must be paid to the way in which AMs apply perception/reasoning to problems/opportunities within their districts.

DEVELOPING AM EXPERTISE

- **Domain Knowledge**
  - Systems/standards training/testing
    - procedures and policies
    - reportage and metrics
  - Immersion
    - OTJ/'back to the floor' training and development
    - 'strawberry patches'/cluster responsibilities for AM potentials

- **Numeracy/Professional Practice**
    - Numerical/cognitive perception/reasoning training
    - case studies and exercises that encompass:
    - portfolio/unit data (quantitative/qualitative) gathering/sifting
    - location of insights/causal drivers
    - patterns of dysfunctionality/opportunity
    - remedial solutions/prioritisation
  - Planning, organising and delegation training
    - portfolio strategy and planning
    - scheduling, meetings and time management ('creating capacity')
    - portfolio delegation

Mastering both elements of expertise will lead to high levels of *judgement* and *confidence* amongst AMs, which will bolster their credibility amongst their peers and followers. The fact remains, however, that whilst most MUEs are good at the former element of expertise (basic domain development), they are generally lax in the latter (numeracy/professional practice), often throwing ex-GMs into the role with little training in diagnostics and problem solving/resolution in complex portfolio situations. Insufficient attention is paid by most MUEs to **cognitive thinking skills** development amongst AMs – a theme to which I will return below.

Case Study 19: Developing Expertise

Adrian Fawcett was previously Group MD of Bass Operating Companies, SVP Acquisitions InBev, COO Punch plc, CEO General Healthcare Group and Chairman of Real Pubs. He is currently Chairman of Park Holidays, Silent Night Group, ARM, Smith Jones Solicitors and Eurosite Power.

… Having run a number of large multi-site organisations, I would say that effective AMs do four things well. First, they get the '*cost of serve–return ratio*' right; that is too say they devote much of their effort and

CONTINUED …

time to areas of their portfolio that will give them the greatest rate of absolute payback. Second, they are adept at expediting what I term *'local KPI fit'*, meaning they disaggregate the key KPIs for specific sites from the 'organisational whole' and apply them rigorously and judiciously at site level within context... focussing upon the different things which relate specifically to each site. Third, they not only attend to the *'midpoint of gravity'* within their portfolios where 'life is comfortable' but also concentrate on the top and bottom ends of their districts, where – for different reasons – the GMs can be disproportionately 'hard work' (possibly 'pushy' at the top end and devoid of capability at the bottom end!). Fourth, they are experts at leveraging a *'virtual central team'* – namely head-office support functions – in order to achieve their objectives. The question is how you develop this expertise amongst AMs... I would point to three facilitating factors:

- *Selection*: AMs should be selected according to their ability to 'problem solve' and 'think critically' about problems/solutions

- *Environment*: It helps if the right organisational culture prevails... allowing AMs to develop tacit expertise in an environment that encourages local experimentation rather than strict conformity

- *Confidence*: Building on the prior point, you tend to find that effective AMs who have tried things that have been successful gain in confidence... a multiplier effect occurs where they emphasise/concentrate upon certain KPIs within specific sites for outcome assurance...

I think it is also important that organisations incentivise AMs intelligently – ensuring that they concentrate on the input–output variables that count... Transparency and simplicity is important... unnecessary caps and complicated over-rider criteria do not drive effective behaviours... often boards and senior leadership fail to apply these common-sense principles when setting incentive schemes! ...

Paul Daynes is the Group HR Director for St Gobain Building Distribution UK and Ireland (Jewson, Grahams, Minster, International Timber), the UK's largest builders' merchants (over 1,000 units). Previously, he held senior positions with Musgrave (Budgens, Londis, SuperValu) and BP Forecourt Retail.

CONTINUED ...

... The three areas of expertise required by AMs are as follows:

- *Compliance*: Technical knowledge of policy, procedures, systems and 'legals'
- *Business development*: P&L interpretation of trends and require-ments of different business segments combined with the ability to prioritise, plan and implement
- *People development*: Ability to match the right GM to the right site and coach them to achieve optimal outcomes without constant reference to higher authorities for 'the answer'.

In my experience, however, AMs (most of whom originate from GM positions) tend to be good at compliance (given their technical training and origins) but less good at business/people development. The reasons for this are threefold... *First*, AMs promoted into the role having been outstanding GMs have been used to direct control of a unit where they 'lead the line' and provide most of the answers... now they have a wide span of control they must manage 'through their people' not 'manage every unit'; a subtle difference... *Second*, after about nine months in retail (perhaps two years in merchanting) because they 'run out of answers' they 'hit the wall'... only those brave enough to ask for help are likely to get through... *Third*, the thinking patterns that AMs deployed as GMs are not sufficient at this level... they must learn to become more analytical and more organised in terms of following things through at a distance... [S]o how do you develop the more tacit skills associated with business/people development?

- *Smaller districts*: I am not an advocate of just giving newly promoted AMs 'strawberry districts' because they tend to manage every unit as if it were their own and can get away with this... crashing and burning when the span becomes greater... Rather, I am an advocate of giving them slightly smaller districts upon which to 'cut their teeth'.
- *Coaching and 'hand-holding'*: Regional directors/HR will devote a great deal of time to coaching AMs to create:
  - 'Secondary structures': At unit level GMs have tightly defined store structures... At district level the AM has a large number

CONTINUED ...

of direct reports… [W]hat the best ones are taught to do is create a '*secondary structure*' on both a geographical (i.e. hub and spoke) and process basis (i.e. service, sales, stocks, compliance champions)… GMs actually welcome these kinds of secondary responsibilities… The benefit of creating these structures is the degree to which they '*free up capacity*' for the AM to do added-value activities such as coaching and business development…

- 'Store accountability': At first the newly promoted GM will try to answer/solve all their stores issues/problems… by being coached to ask the question 'what do you think?' back to the GM, they lessen dependence levels… again, opening up capacity to do other things… [A]lthough most newly appointed AMs will have an opinion on most of the questions they are asked, they really must 'stop giving their GMs the answers' if they are to have any capacity for action…

- *Analytical provision*: Outstanding AMs will take an analytical approach to problems/opportunities; for instance, if feedback from customers in a particular branch points to the fact that the local market lacks landscaping provision, they will carry out a proper market analysis and trial/pilot a limited amount of product in a defined space before 'scaling up'… However, this kind of approach is unusual in 'do then think' operators, so we have put well-qualified business analysts into the business who provide our AMs with 'back up' (sizing local markets, pricing, phased approaches etc.)…

The final point I would make about these latter two development interventions is that AMs require the right *mindset/degree of humility* to learn, ask questions and adapt… After a period of time – as they become more successful – their levels of tacit knowledge and confidence will grow… but the good ones will always seek to acquire new and better ways of doing things! …

THREE KEY 'EXPERTISE' QUESTIONS FOR AM DEVELOPERS

1. Have you got sufficient training in place so that your AMs can 'read the P&L'? (NOT JUST THE 'OUTPUT' NUMBERS – THEIR 'INPUT' DEPENDENCIES AS WELL!)

2. Are your AMs trained in 'distance-based' managerial skills: planning, prioritising, organising, supervising projects and delegating *at a distance*? (Their capability in this area will give them extra time/capacity TO LEAD AND INSPIRE.)

3. Do you regularly check their technical skills to ensure they are relevant and up-to-date? (For instance, in food service: food production and service delivery.)

EMOTIONAL INTELLIGENCE

Given the importance of the human dimension of MUEs, with their heavy operational reliance on labour and frequent B2C interactions, it is unsurprising that the second major characteristic of effective AMs is emotional intelligence (EI). This is defined generally within the academic literature as an ability, skill or perceived ability to identify, assess and control the emotions of oneself, others and groups (Goleman 1998). This characteristic – which comprises three dimensions including *self-control and mental toughness*, follower *insight and exchange* and *relationship management* – will now be considered, followed by illustrations as to how it might be developed.

SELF-AWARENESS AND MENTAL TOUGHNESS

The combination of 'knowing oneself' and exercising personal control through high levels of mental toughness is an important feature of effective AMs. Due to the workload and associated pressures/stresses of the role, effective MULs need to acquire a degree of self-knowledge and discipline with regards to how they react to certain situations, demonstrating a fair amount of 'manners and grace under immense provocation'. Effective AMs demonstrate the following behaviours with regards to self-awareness and mental toughness:

FACETS OF SELF-AWARENESS AND MENTAL TOUGHNESS

- Self-awareness through:
  - honest reflection
  - desire for improvement
  - ability to listen to feedback
- Mental toughness through:
  - adapting to different challenges and circumstances
  - emotional self-control under pressure
  - balanced view of success and failure
  - focus upon controlling the 'controllables'
  - confidence in one's own abilities.

FOLLOWER INSIGHT AND EXCHANGE

Self-awareness will undoubtedly help the AM – through the process of understanding 'self' – to read the motives/desires of their followers, guiding them as to which practices/approaches they should adopt with individuals/teams to induce reciprocity and indebtedness so that they can rely on high levels of operational excellence without direct daily supervision. With regard to awareness of others – in order to shape and control emotions – effective AMs display the following attributes:

FACETS OF FOLLOWER INSIGHT

- Empathy: authentic questioning and listening skills
- Processing: ability to 'read/interpret the motives of others'
- 'Fit': ability to apply right 'currency of exchange'.

Based on my previous research, this ability to gain follower insight is a skill that is more evident in female rather than male AMs. The ability to sense, understand and respond to the emotions/motives of others did not come naturally to a number of output-focused male AMs. Their tendency to 'talk at' their people rather than listening and empathising was a major inhibiting factor in gaining control of the emotions of others. This is a major inhibitor. Whilst the AM's capacity to understand the attitudes, disposition and motivations of his or her followers – in order to lead to them achieving assured operational outcomes – is an important entry point, it is the AM's skill in adapting/fitting the right exchange mechanisms to the right person/team that will ultimately determine value-added reciprocity-based behaviour:

FACETS OF FOLLOWER EXCHANGE

- Understand – locate follower needs/desires through:
  - listening to 'stories' and observing real behaviours/outcomes
- Apply 'guile' and 'nous' – 'fit' currencies of exchange through:
  - judging personality, attitude, capability and situation
  - ensure the *costs* of follower roles are compensated by *benefits* that lead to positive *outcomes* (benefits–costs=outcomes)
  - create 'win–win' solutions for both the AM and GM
- Monitor outcomes – constantly review desired outputs:
  - operational excellence without direct daily supervision.

RELATIONSHIP AND CONFLICT MANAGEMENT

As stated, it is the natural inclination of many AMs to 'go native', disassociating themselves from the rest of the wider organisation in the misplaced belief that it is 'out to get them'. Such a position is not only immature and ultimately self-defeating; it also has a negative impact on performance by closing off access to valuable information and potential support mechanisms. Thus, in addition to self-awareness and follower insight, effective AMs are adept at fostering and maintaining good relationships across the organisation. Effective AMs are able to deal with ambiguity, understanding that most organisations are riven by competing interests and that they can only control the 'controllables'. In the absence of having the power and influence to prevent conflict between the operational line and, for instance, parts of the technocracy such as Property or Marketing, they focus upon getting the very best outcomes possible in difficult situations. Within their own orbit of control, they use the techniques and methods outlined above, the most significant weapon being the creation of 'win–win' outcomes through the process of social exchange with support staff:

FACETS OF RELATIONSHIP AND CONFLICT MANAGEMENT

- Creation of 'enabling' networks through:
  - spending time at the centre (either job role or networking)
  - telephoning and meeting peers
  - volunteering for project work and task forces
- Transparency and honesty during dealings (limiting game play)
- Asking for help/involving others in solutions (recognising their contribution)
- Creating 'win–win' situations through social exchange (help support staff attain own goals).

DEVELOPING AM EI

How do MUEs develop EI amongst AMs? Changing or modifying behaviours which are connected to personality and prior socialisation is notoriously difficult, unless the recipients are open to honest feedback which they are prepared to incorporate into alternative ways of working. MUEs can help AMs to understand their levels of resilience/self-control and their impact upon others (followers, peers and stakeholders) but it is individual preparedness to change which is key:

DEVELOPING AM EMOTIONAL INTELLIGENCE

- Measure current position:
  - 360 degree, MTQ48, observation, previous data (PDP feedback, Employee Engagement etc.)
- Behavioural interventions:
  - coaching/mentoring
  - field-based observation and feedback
  - modelling from exemplars
  - classroom simulation
  - reflective logs
  - placement on central project teams/secondments/rotation.

Case Study 20: Developing Emotional Intelligence

Deborah Kemp is the CEO of Laurel (a funeral-parlour chain), having previously been CEO of De Vere Hotels and COO of Punch plc.

... Having acquired technical knowledge it is essential that our area managers and funeral directors display high levels of emotional intelligence... This is because in our business customer service ('doing it right') is not enough – making sure the customer experience ('doing the right thing') exceeds expectations is key... [S]uccess in this business is highly contingent upon local recommendation and advocacy... So how do our people 'connect' with our customers? ... The way they achieve this is, first, by exercising high levels of empathy and listening skills... establishing what the customer really wants... listening to their stories and reminiscences... Second, our people have to be adept at managing conflict – understanding and resolving issues concerning funeral arrangements that might arise between family members... To reinforce these behaviours, our area managers have to both manage and lead... *manage* the transactional aspects of the business (due procedure and compliance)... lead from a transformational perspective; reinforcing good behaviour by instilling confidence amongst their followers... praising, reinforcing and recognising behaviours that enhance the customer experience (making people *feel* well looked after)... In order to achieve this level of customer intimacy the best AMs 'tap into' their people... understanding their needs and motivations; adapting their style and approach accordingly... From a practical point of view, we enhance levels of EI in the business through role-play exercises (simulating various 'touch points' during the customer journey) and group discussions where AMs and funeral directors are asked 'when and why did you get really good feedback from a customer'... [F]ocusing on the positives (as opposed to the negatives) gives people confidence to try always to do the 'right thing' for the customer...

CONTINUED ...

Adrian Fawcett was previously Group MD of Bass Operating Companies, SVP Acquisitions InBev, COO Punch plc, CEO General Healthcare Group and Chairman of Real Pubs. He is currently Chairman of Park Holidays, Silent Night Group, ARM, Smith Jones Solicitors and Eurosite Power.

... In my experience, AMs who display great EI are very perceptive regarding personalities, capabilities and situations... The way in which they will get things done – through a sophisticated process of *reciprocation* – means that they will have ensured that 'x, y and z will be completed' by the next time they visit... [T]hrough such means [bargaining and reciprocation] I believe that effective AMs *cannot be regarded as 'remote' managers*, because they have – through a number of vehicles – created strong practical and emotional connections with their followers! ... Another insight that I would offer is that effective AMs rarely 'leave their GMs on the floor' when they leave – whatever the substance of the discussion... there is always a 'pick me up' at the end that leaves a motivational last impression... Also, good AMs need to be 'emotionally' comfortable as mobile workers; often ex-fixed-site operators fail to cope emotionally with high degrees of distance and detachment from daily/hourly doses of close human interaction and the vicarious nature of their roles... Finally, you tend to find that good AMs are aware that retail is about emotion – engaging people through fun, anecdotes, wit and humour will always win over dry 'rationalism'! ... Are such attributes taught or innate? ... I would argue that they are a combination of the two, but organisations can certainly help AMs raise their own self-awareness regarding their impact upon others through a variety of techniques alongside selecting AMs who have some semblance of EI in the first place! ... After all, we are talking about people businesses here... 'people work for people' not just organisations!

THREE KEY 'EMOTIONAL INTELLIGENCE' QUESTIONS FOR AM DEVELOPERS

1. Is your AM population 'self-aware'; that is to say, do they know what their dominant personality type/leadership styles are and the effect they have on their followers?

2. Do your AMs have the appropriate recruitment, coaching, exchange and motivational skills to lead at a distance in a B2C business environment? (Check they are capable of spotting GM 'winners' and exchanging with followers – deploying the 'right currencies, with the right people, at the right time' so that they achieve operational excellence without direct daily supervision!)

3. Do your AMs have the *nous* and *guile* to manage inter-personal conflict and *negotiate* their way through difficult situations? (Managing people out of units – without recourse to formal means – is an art and a science!)

ENTREPRENEURSHIP

The next characteristic that effective AMs display is corporate entrepreneurship where – within a given framework – they focus relentlessly upon doing things 'quicker, smarter and better'. Classically, corporate innovators have been termed 'intrapreneurs', implying that – given existing constraints – they think and act differently from their non-corporate 'maverick' entrepreneurial cousins. This is manifestly not the case. The kind of behaviours that entrepreneurs display – constant challenging of orthodoxy and a courageous desire to create something innovative – are characteristics that are shared by corporate entrepreneurs, albeit that the latter have to innovate in more bounded environments. Indeed, one advantage that corporate entrepreneurs have is the 'hard' and 'soft' resources to trial new products and methods of working. Obviously, their job is made easier if organisations recognise the benefits of 'bottom-up' innovation, creating 'space' for NPD and encouraging/capturing value-added insights through feedback loops and recognition. But what dimensions of entrepreneurship apply to AMs? What are the sub-components needed for its successful exposition?

COURAGE AND CURIOSITY

In both 'hard' and 'soft' branded MUEs, it is an incontrovertible fact that, due to a number of legacy-related and/or contextual factors, almost *every site is different*. Sites are rarely *completely* homogenous in terms of position, scale, layout, officialdom, customer demographics and labour markets. This represents a major opportunity for the effective AM to make local alterations (where permissible) to processes, configuration, offer, range, pricing, promotions, local PR and rates of pay in order to leverage sales. In order to do this, however, the effective MSM needs appropriate levels of *curiosity* which enable him/her to '**see the differences**'. In addition, (s)he needs the appropriate level of *courage* and *relentless persistence* to drive/permit *legal* improvements (i.e. adaptations that are not going to 'blow up the machine' or result in 'gorging') both in single sites and across the portfolio.

FACETS OF AM COURAGE AND CURIOSITY

- Courage to try new things:
  - 'don't ask for permission, ask for forgiveness'
- Natural inquisitiveness about:
  - how well things work for staff *and* customers!
  - how things can be done better to reduce costs or increase sales!
- Ability to 'SEE THE DIFFERENCES' in each site:
  - i.e. processes, layout, range, promotion, events (social media)

TRANSMISSION AND IMPLEMENTATION

The difficulty facing naturally innovative and inquisitive AMs is how they take added-value ideas that emerge from one unit and 'land' them across their portfolios. For sure, they can assign responsibility for knowledge transfer and delivery to their nominated process champions and leads but how do they facilitate more 'organic' means of transmission/adoption? The answer to this is that effective AMs will encourage knowledge transference across their portfolios by breaking 'hoarding' behaviours (i.e. the posses-sors of useful knowledge refusing to share insights due to their competitive advantage) through encouraging reciprocity and universal mutual gain.

The forum through which such 'sharing' can be encouraged and engineered (particularly in managed/franchised environments) is during district meetings where effective AMs, having dealt with the 'compliance stuff' (i.e. labour, other costs, and health and safety) during weekly teleconference/Skype calls, will concentrate on improvement and innovation.

FACETS OF TRANSMISSION AND IMPLEMENTATION

- Process capability to deliver and 'land' things
  - utilise process 'leads' and 'champions'
- Knowledge transfer mechanisms to break 'hoarding'
  - events, conferences, rotations, placements, 'sitting-with-nellie', communities of practice (clusters etc.)

DEVELOPING AM ENTREPRENEURSHIP

How do MUEs encourage entrepreneurship amongst their AM population? AMs have generally been promoted from GM level for their technical proficiency rather than cognitive thinking skills. Additionally, those that have been genuinely innovative in-store have usually not been responsible for spreading ideas over distance, across a portfolio of sites (unless they have been assigned to do so). What MUEs need to do, therefore, is to ensure their AM population has a sufficient level of courage and critical thinking to 'try new things', in addition to understanding the mechanisms through which they can encourage cross-portfolio knowledge transmission.

DEVELOPING AM ENTREPENEURSHIP

- Senior role-modelling:
  - construction/demonstrations of 'freedom within a frame'
  - public recognition of innovation/process improvement
  - permission to try and fail (remove penalties/sanctions)
- Measure AM current position:
  - psychometric profiling (MINDSET, curiosity, persistence and courage), previous evidence of innovating/risk taking, problem solving skills
- Development interventions:

- brainstorming tools/OPI (Operational Improvement and Innovation) techniques/case study examples
- portfolio knowledge-transfer training:
  - process leads and champions, meetings and events etc.
- Impact and influencing skills training:
  - how to transmit ideas upwards to senior policy makers

Case Study 21: Developing Entrepreneurship

Peter Howe is Director of Learning and Development EMEA for Coffee Shop (both pseudonyms) previously having held HRD and consultancy roles in a number of multi-site businesses.

... A major observation I'd make about successful area managers in multi-site operations is that the best ones do seem to display higher levels of curiosity and courage than the rest... When you examine closely why many of the top area managers outperform the rest, you tend to find that constantly they challenge their teams around 'how can we sell more, faster?' ... In coffee shops, driving the number of transactions per hour at peak (breakfast and lunch) is key – as is filling 'non-peak' shoulder sessions around lunch... With regards to increasing transactions per hour at peak, good AMs will ensure that their store teams are sufficiently trained in terms of customer order, production and queue management (remember, in the coffee business 45% of transactions relate to two products: cappuccinos and lattes)... Indeed, they will often get onto the line to model best behaviours (interacting with customers who are patiently waiting down the queue with comments like 'be with you in a minute sir/madam!') ... [T]hey will also be adept at spotting pinch points within certain stores (due to estate expansion issues, few are exactly the same): can kit be moved around for better flows? ... will promotions require different product layout? ... can impulse purchases be put in better positions? ... Also, with regard to non-peak sessions, good AMs will ask themselves which consumer groups in which micro-markets should be targeted to 'fill the gaps' (young mothers, student 'grazers', snacking shoppers)...

CONTINUED ...

[A]lso, which events/promotions will fit which groups at what times? … Although segmentation at a company level will provide some solutions, good AMs will also feedback ideas and insights from a local level so that standardised interventions (i.e. apps, Facebook, e-mail and digital marketing) drive traffic more effectively… How do you develop this kind of local innovation and knowledge creation amongst the AM population? … Strong senior role models that 'encourage rather than punish'… selecting 'reflective' and courageous AMs in the first place… providing enough 'corporate slack' for some kind of innovation… praise and recognition for people who 'think outside the box' to produce solutions that drive sales!

Paul Daynes is the Group HR Director for St Gobain Building Distribution UK and Ireland (Jewson, Grahams, Minster, International Timber), the UK's largest builders' merchants (over 1,000 units). Previously, he held senior positions with Musgrave (Budgens, Londis, SuperValu) and BP Forecourt Retail.

… For me, the best AMs display entrepreneurship in three ways… *First*, they are adept at what I term *improvement* activities: figuring out the best customer flows and most efficient ergonomics – spotting how on-site hard and soft resources can be leveraged more effectively to improve throughputs, yields and capacity utilisation… *Second*, they engage in *innovation*; particularly with regard to sales… in this sense they are adept at increasing the range/offer that penetrates other customer segments within local micro-markets… increasing footfall and traffic… *Third* – and particularly importantly – they do not just have 'good ideas' – they are expert at 'landing' them and diffusing them across their portfolios… How do they do this? … With regard to *implementation* they generally have strong project management skills (what, by whom, when and review)… In relation to getting people to *share ideas* and try out new things, they have built up strong relational/emotional ties (quickly) with their GMs who are inclined to trust their judgement… these ties have been built up through close 'personal emotional' attachments being formed through the AM being attuned to the needs of individuals, quick to honour promises and standing behind their people when times are tough… The question arises, however, as to why few AMs

CONTINUED …

consistently demonstrate such behaviours... This is connected to the sectoral specificity of their skills... [M]any AMs are risk averse to 'giving it a go' because unlike generalists – such as HR, finance and property professionals – they cannot move sectors... in order to keep their jobs, they play it safe... So how do you develop the attributes of corporate entrepreneurship amongst AMs? First, pick ones with the right attitudes, behaviours and mindsets (curiosity, courage, authenticity and humility) and, second, provide an environment in which it is alright to try things and fail...

THREE KEY 'ENTREPRENEURSHIP' QUESTIONS FOR AM DEVELOPERS

1. Have you created a culture in which AMs with high levels of courage and curiosity can flourish? (You should clearly specify areas for 'freedom within a frame'.)

2. Are your AMs equipped (through technical insight and cognitive reasoning) to 'see the differences' at a local level and make improvements that will add manifest value?

3. Do you have sufficient systems in place to allow AMs to share their insights with peers, decision makers and support staff?

ENERGY

Expertise, EI and entrepreneurship are critical components in the makeup of the effective AM but they will be diluted, potentially rendered irrelevant, unless individuals have high energy levels. Given the aforementioned challenges and stresses of the role – derived from geographical, span of control and positional pressures – effective AMs require significant reserves of energy to overcome 'interference' in order to get the job done. What are the critical dimensions of this construct with regards to AMs?

STAMINA

The 24/7 nature of the AM role dictates that they must have high levels of stamina/'installed capacity' to work in order to cope with its demands. In academic terms, stamina or physical energy is typically defined as the ability to sustain a prolonged physical or mental effort. Rituals such as nutrition, exercise, sleep and rest have a positive correlation with increased work capacity, engagement and motivation. Such habits are regarded by some commentators as among the most effective behaviours for controlling and reducing stressors. The reality, however, is that given the demands and intractable conundrums faced on a day-to-day basis by most AMs, few have the time or space to achieve physical or spiritual balance. Whilst a limited amount of stress is seen as a useful performance enhancer in certain circumstances, constant burdensome demands for the AM can sap stamina, eventually leading to declining levels of discretionary effort, high intention-to-quit rates and, in extreme cases, absence, sickness and burn out.

But why do AMs require such large reserves of stamina?

FACTORS REQUIRING AM STAMINA

- Physical distance with units
- BAU activity execution:
  - operational excellence
  - application of professional practice
- Ad hoc initiatives:
  - organisation change
  - refurbishments and new openings
  - product pilots/launches
  - troubleshooting/firefighting

There is little doubt that the AM role, with its large amount of sedentary travel between units and unusual working hours, can promote an exceptionally unhealthy lifestyle. Why? In part, the answer lies in the addictive nature of the job, the fact that AMs become, in the words of one respondent, 'e-mail junkies and iPhone addicts'. To a certain extent, the addictive nature of the job (where there is no end to the number of tasks that need completing or problems that require resolution) provides constant affirmation of their identity – proving that they are needed and important!

PASSION AND PACE

MUEs are 'people' businesses where AMs need to convey infectious enthusiasm and a 'can do' attitude that engages and motivates their staff, who – in turn – will enthuse their customers. Within the academic literature, *passion* is typically conceived as *personal commitment*, high levels of which are thought to be achieved through job role 'fit', goal alignment and HRM practice interventions (i.e. development, reward, communication and involvement). It is also linked to levels of *positive energy*, which is conceptualised as being able to help people to perform at their best through techniques such as 'expressing appreciation to others', thereby fuelling 'positive emotions' (Schwartz 2007). In addition, conveying passion is inextricably linked to *pace* and urgency. Given the service orientation of MUEs, where front-line staff are expected to respond immediately and sympathetically to customer demands, effective AMs set the 'dynamic tone' by dispatching tasks and requests quickly and efficiently. The importance of pace is recognised by academic commentators, most notably Belbin (2000) who argued that organisations and teams require 'completer finishers' (a prime requirement of field-based operatives in MUEs) alongside other actors, in order to ensure that tasks are implemented on time, to specification.

FACETS BEHIND PASSION AND PACE

- Passion and 'emotional contagion' through:
  - humour, fun and enjoyment
  - infectious enthusiasm
  - cheerleading success
  - visibility and positivity
  - 'changing gears' (according to season, event, trading session etc.)
- Pace and urgency through:
  - anticipating and acting upon issues swiftly
  - quick responses to requests (promissory speed)
  - progress chasing/implementation
  - answering e-mails and smartphone messages regularly
  - following up on promises
  - turning around work swiftly and efficiently

Going back to passion, it is important to state that its conveyance has positive effects both ways. AMs derive much of their inspiration and energy from the passion of their people: site visits often serve an AM's need to be re-energised. Given the somewhat isolated home-working environment of their role and the stifling demands of the centre, AMs often find site visits refreshing and motivational. Seeing the positive outcomes of appointments that they have made and the successes of their people reinforces their sense of passion for the job.

DEVELOPING AM ENERGY

Inevitably, individual reserves of AM energy are connected to work ethic, attitude, personality and situation (i.e. the ebb and flow of central dictats and demands). But what can MUEs do to develop and enhance levels of energy?

DEVELOPING AM ENERGY

- Measure current position:
  - personal productivity (level/speed of tasks despatched, number of store visits etc.)
  - staff engagement and customer satisfaction
- Behavioural interventions:
  - 'wellness' programmes
    - medical check-ups
    - rules on work hours, travel, smartphones and laptop/tablet use
  - managerial skills training (creating capacity)
    - planning, prioritisating, organising and delegating
- Technical interventions:
  - architecture
    - store numbers and geography
    - nominated support staff support
  - process efficiency
    - machinery, technology and facilities that work
    - procedural and process SIMPLICITY
    - appropriate staff-training systems

Case Study 22: Developing Energy

Steve Cash was a brand operations director for Mitchells and Butlers having run a number of brands including Crown Carveries and Vintage Inns.

... Great AMs need plenty of energy – particularly when they take over a new district... One of the common misconceptions of effective area management is that one of the first things AMs should do is deal with the poor performers in the district... This is misguided... What the best AMs tend to do is create good relationships with the top performers in the district to build up trust and 'lock them in'... the message that the effective AM is transmitting to the key personnel in the district is 'you are important and I value your contribution... I want to work with you... I need your help!' ... After all, the poor performers will have been 'problems' for some time and cannot be shifted overnight unless they are on a performance plan (which in itself is a long, painstaking process)... Also, going in heavy-handedly – ignoring the efforts of the superior operators and concentrating solely on those with attitude/skills issues – will unsettle many of the good guys who will perceive the AM as being 'punishment orientated'... Eventually, the good AM, having *'over-indexed'* with their superior operators, will either have convinced the rest to follow suit or encouraged them to leave... the tipping point is over 50% buy-in to what the AM is trying to by effective operators in the district... By year three on the district, good AMs are usually 'motoring'... However, covering all the bases requires high levels of stamina and persistence... travelling inordinate amounts of physical distance to be seen 'on the ground'... In terms of getting hold of good people, great AMs will also spend at least 25% of their time on recruitment, training and coaching – in itself both physically and emotionally energy-sapping... If they can get to a position (particularly in hospitality) where they have put in place a stable team of high performers, they are likely to do well... How do you develop this energy amongst AMs? ... [P]artly it is down to horsepower but also good planning/prioritisation skills and high levels of passion/belief on the part of the AM...

THREE KEY 'ENERGY' QUESTIONS FOR AM DEVELOPERS

1. Do your AMs have a high 'installed capacity' to work? (Make sure you protect their energy levels by 'cutting the crap' from policy makers.)
2. Are your AMs passionate about their jobs and 'emotionally contagious' with their people?
3. Do your AMs despatch tasks and initiatives within their districts with vigour and pace?

ETHICS

The field of business ethics (a phrase that, in the current climate, seems somewhat oxymoronic!) has received considerable attention over the past few years in developed contexts. This is not least due to the dubious behaviours of bankers that contributed to the 2008 financial collapse in the 'West', which occurred in spite of previous attempts by policy makers to instil legal codes of permitted behaviour (i.e. Sarbannes Oxley 'financial disclosure' regulations in the United States, put in place post-Enron). MUEs like other corporate entities all have CSR and compliance frameworks which define rights and obligations that should govern relations between themselves and their stakeholders. In particular, employees are prescribed ethical obligations to their organisations (i.e. reporting malfeasance through whistleblowing). The issue in MUEs is how – given the dispersed multi-site nature of the organisational entity – organisations are able to regulate behaviours effectively. In this respect, they are highly reliant on their field-based personnel AMs to conform to their codes of ethics.

The foundation of ethical behaviour is sound *morals*, namely: the ability to act 'properly' in a 'good' way. Essentially, individual morality is derived from ethical 'social mores' enshrined in *societal* and cultural *values*. Previous reference has been made to how values are imprinted upon individuals through conditioning and socialisation at a very early age through parenting, education and peer-group influences. There are two issues for AMs – first, how do they ensure their own *personal morality* is aligned to that of the MUE and, second, how do they influence and regulate the *value-sets* of those around them?

As regards the first question, AMs in MUEs will sometimes be placed in situations where they are faced with seemingly intractable decisions. Given their distance from the centre and the demands placed upon them to hit certain financial targets, should they cheat (i.e. bribe officials or falsify data/accounts) to get ahead? Also – in certain high-context cultures – should they accede to local customs, favouring relationships above performance, and asserting their authority in a 'self-protective' manner? Here, the unlearning of poor practice, and self-regulation and *moral control* amongst AMs are particularly important if they are 'to do the right thing'. In respect of others, the AM has a huge role to play in modelling MUE *values* – especially in relation to followers. For instance, Generation Y and (upcoming) 'Millennials' are portrayed as having different aspirations and value sets from previous generations. Their conception of work is less 'dutiful cradle to grave', more 'means to and end' – work providing income for extra-curricular social activities. The AM, therefore, has a key role in ensuring that the value sets of MUEs are inculcated into younger workers who are not conditioned to accept some quite basic norms (i.e. standards, timekeeping, appearance, behaviour etc.).

FACETS OF AM ETHICS

- 'Doing the right thing' as well as 'doing it right'
- Acting authentically through:
  - consistent, balanced and mature behaviours
  - honest and open communications
- Fairness and equity through:
  - no favouritism/nepotism
  - balanced adjudication on misdemeanours

DEVELOPING AM ETHICS

The issue for MUEs is how to ensure their values 'transcend' personal/ local cultural values where there are clear disjunctures. More specifically, how can they ensure their AMs have sufficiently robust moral compasses and that their organisational values are accepted and enacted by individuals who might be conditioned to operate according to a contrary set of values (especially amongst Generation Y workers)?

HOW TO DEVELOP AM ETHICS

- Measure current position:
  - test ethics through psychometrics
  - analyse patterns of previous decision making
  - check on previous behaviour; talk to subordinates – analyse employee engagement scores on trust
  - observe during a 'trial' period of employment
- Interventions:
  - modelling; socialisation through 'leader' values modelling
  - benefit upselling; sell the upsides (i.e. how organisational values result in positive personal outcomes for individuals in terms of meritocratic progression, reputation etc.)
  - coherent logic: ensure 'coherent logic' prevails for value set

Case Study 23: Developing Ethics

Deborah Kemp is the CEO of Laurel (a funeral-parlour chain), having previously been CEO of De Vere Hotels and COO of Punch plc.

… When I took over this business a couple of years ago, we instituted a set of values that would bind together an 'organisational family' from what had been a pretty disparate set of businesses operating under different names throughout the UK… I wanted a set of values that would act as a parameter/'moral compass' for this business so that people would understand what we stood for and what was/wasn't permissible outside of usual processes, whilst still retaining the local identity and personality of our businesses… The values we have embedded in the business are *trust* (we will back our people to do the right thing for the customer), *responsive* (24/7 customer responsiveness), *accessible* (customers can come and talk to us before and after the funeral), *respectful* (tailoring our approach to customer needs) and *progressive* (we are not stuck in the past)… These values are constantly reinforced through behavioural modelling by myself and the senior leadership

CONTINUED …

team... also through constant reinforcement through purposefully 'weaving it into the language' of the business... Whilst some values – such as *progressive* – have been difficult for some colleagues to get a handle on, I find that by bringing them alive through stories, metaphors and anecdotes helps transmission... Also, bundling up customer feedback around the values really helps (a comment like 'you were open to my ideas' is aligned to the *progressive* value)... Furthermore, improving the quality of our marketing and amenity (making our parlours more *accessible* through removing window blinds, altering layouts, better lighting and background music) is a clear physical reinforcement to our people that our values matter...

Nick Rowe is the Chairman of pod, a London-based chain of fast 'ethical/health' 'food-to-go' restaurants. Previously, he worked in a senior capacity in American Express and Diners Club.

... After eight years working with a founder entrepreneur and his management team trying patiently to build a differentiated brand with a clear positioning, I would offer the following insights on ethics... *First*, the product itself must be authentic and ethical... At pod we have worked hard to position ourselves as a nutritional spicy 'food-to-go' offer aimed principally at City office workers... but with strong ethical sourcing and production values... For instance we source the finest ingredients for hot and cold food with distinctive health properties (green Thai curries and 'detox' boxes) and invite customers to divide their waste into packaged and compostable... [O]ur brand really taps into aspirational GenY customers who want to look after both their bodies and the world around them... *Second*, it is important that I and the team 'live the values' of the brand... when I took over as Chairman, I must have made forty-odd store visits in a short space of time and also hosted a get-together between the store managers and board which went down really well with the troops... Although the aim of the board is to optimise returns for investors – eventually (hopefully) devising some kind of profit-able exit for our principal backers... it is important that we preserve the ethical DNA of who we are and what we do through all our actions... I do not see capital and ethics as being uncomfortable bedfellows... you just have to ensure that people do not lose their

CONTINUED ...

compasses when things are going well… behavioural restraint over matters such as pay and bonuses is important because the over-riding objective of people working in this brand should not be 'how do I get rich quick?' but 'how do we build something meaningful, sustainable and then (ultimately) profitable?!' …

THREE KEY 'ETHICS' QUESTIONS FOR AM DEVELOPERS

1. Do you have a clear statement of values that explains 'the way in which we do business/treat people around here'?
2. Do you measure AMs against these values/ethics when you recruit them?
3. Are your AMs educated/socialised to understand that the positive values *they* display will lead to value-added intentional/purposeful behaviours at site level? (This is the best 'soft' way of maintaining control at a distance!)

SUMMARY

This chapter began with a comparison between the UM and AM role. This is pertinent because nearly 70% of AMs in MUEs originate from unit-management positions. Factors that were highlighted as being of particular significance included the observation that leader–follower physical distance between the two roles was significantly different, with AMs having a wide span of control (compared to UMs' 'tight' span) and a detachment from day-to-day interaction with customers (UMs being 'close'). A major conse-quence of this lack of proximity is that AMs required the requisite cognitive/behavioural skills to 'think and do' (rather than the 'do then think' required of UMs) in relation to closing down multi-dimensional aspects of distance referred to elsewhere in this book that can potentially derail AMs' impact upon their followers and (consequently) customers.

The previous three chapters highlighted a number of practice-based interventions that AMs deploy (sometimes simultaneously) to 'animate' and manage their portfolios. This chapter has considered the personal characteristics that AMs require to fashion and institute some of these practices, namely expertise, emotional intelligence, energy, entrepreneurism and ethics. Connections were made between these attributes and specific practices, a major insight being that companies wishing to develop these skills needed to concentrate their resources less upon technical matters (these having been largely developed at UM level) but more upon behavioural/cognitive development. Additionally, in light of the principal enquiry of the book – how AMs lead and manage at a distance (which draws upon substantial empirical evidence garnered both for this book and for the two preceding it) – it can be argued that these various attributes can be associated with mitigating the multiple dimensions of the leader–member 'distance problem' outlined in 'Distance Literature' in Chapter 1. Recasting our frame of analysis, the following strong associations can be seen between: expertise and reducing *structural* distance (through delegation, prioritisation and organisation); emotional intelligence and addressing *psychological/social* distance (through follower insight and exchange); and entrepreneurship and the removal of functional (i.e. 'insider' versus 'outsider') barriers to knowledge transmission (through the application of 'sharing' mechanisms/forums). Thus, whilst in a normative sense the personal characteristics required by AMs can be seen as enabling effective professional practice, they can also be viewed in a wider perspective as facilitating 'proximal' leadership through solving (consciously or unconsciously) the multi-variant distance issues posed by the role.

CHAPTER 8
CONCLUSION

This book is a modest attempt to outline the practices of professional area management. Unlike my previous books on multi-site managers, it has taken more of a practical approach, highlighting key tools and techniques that can be utilised by AMs to improve their performance. It was important, however, to ensure that academic rigour unpinned the whole endeavour – hence the use of empirical data from my previous two books (Edger 2012, 2013) and case-study illustrations. But – aside from a description of what the essential practices of professional AMs are – what is the key insight of *this* book with regards to the role and its successful execution? What further observation does this book make, building upon the contributions of the first two volumes on effective area management?

The sub-title of this book, *Leading at a Distance in Multi-Unit Enterprises*, gives the reader a clue as to one of the main inhibitors in executing the AM role: distance. Indeed, this problem and the ways in which effective AMs overcome it resonate throughout the book – particularly in the summaries to each chapter. This final chapter will attempt to bring all the strands together by arguing that, rather than being a one-dimensional construct – as many scholars operating in the multi-unit management domain assume – *distance is multi-faceted*. Thus, whilst the narratives contained in this book validate Umbreit's (1989) observation that 'managing at a distance' is *the* major challenge facing effective AMs, further contemplation/triangulation of the narratives and data suggest that what effective AMs do is to 'close down' *three* principal variants of distance – *structural*, *psychological* and *functional* – through the application of the specific practices that are outlined within this book. This conclusion will therefore offer up two major contributions that are designed to take the study of the area-management domain further: first, by offering a better conceptualisation of distance within a multi-site context; and second, with reference to practice-based applications, by discussing how it is dealt with and overcome by professional AMs.

REFRAMING MULTI-SITE DISTANCE

As stated, one issue that surfaces constantly in multi-site management research is this notion of 'distance' being a major constraint to the reali-sation of operational excellence (Fox 2014). Indeed, my writings and the ground-breaking research of scholars such as Umbreit (1989) clearly make the empirical observation that – sitting in the middle of the MUEs – AMs frequently express high levels of anxiety about their isolation and detach-ment from both the centre and their units! But what myself and others have failed to define is what distance *means*, what its *consequences* are, and how AMs *overcome* it – even if I implied in my first book that AMs 'get closer' to their units through '*local leadership*' (engendering GM stability/motivation through '*local HRM*' and reciprocal exchanges) and to the centre by 'insight' and 'enabling' networking.

What emerges from this book, however, is a validation of the multi-faceted definition of distance (particularly that of Napier and Ferris 1993) that allows it to be conceived of in *structural*, *psychological* and *functional* terms. Furthermore, these forms of distance contextualise the professional practice of AMs – something that will be dealt with in the next section. But what are these nascent classifications of distance and why do they act as such formidable barriers to AMs? Each construct and its respective sub-components will now be reprised by turn.

- **Structural Distance**: This comprises two elements – physical and hierarchical – which both provide formidable barriers to the execution of the AM role.
  - *Physical distance*: Given the dispersed nature of their port-folios, AMs are geographically/spatially detached from their units. The time that they spend travelling around their units – exacerbated in many cases by their huge span of control (sometimes up to 32 units) – limits the amount of time that they can spend in a store organising, supervising and under-standing its idiosyncratic micro-market, context-specific and staff-based needs. In particular, physical distance limits the frequency and intensity of interactions (essential for building deep-seated, trusting relationships) – a major rate-limiter given the people-centric nature of MUEs in general.
  - *Hierarchical distance*: Situated in the middle of the organisa-tion, the AM position occupies a space between the strategic apex/technocracy and the units. Hence, the AM is tasked by

the centre to expedite a number of (sometimes irreconcilable) tasks and duties whilst dealing with the 'kickback' from the branch management teams when/if poorly conceived dictats and policies flow through the line. This positional distance is accentuated because, in some MUEs, policy makers fail to co-opt the views and skills of AMs in framing initiatives, the view being taken that AMs are mere conduits or implementers. This reinforces the view amongst the AM population itself, and also amongst their teams, that they are detached/separated from the 'body politic' and have little impact and influence within the wider organisation. Another consequence of hierarchical distance, particularly in MUEs with poor communications, is the lack of understanding/buy-in AMs and their teams might have of company strategy and objectives.

- **Psychological Distance**: Partially because of physical distance, but also due to age, experience, values and conditioning, AM effectiveness can be limited by psychological distance. This has two dimensions: demographic and cultural.

  - *Demographic distance*: Understanding and perception of the attitudes, desires and behaviours of their team and their customers can be hampered by 'contaminant' factors such as age and prior experience. Often AMs are older than their unit managers; the degree to which 'baby boomers' or 'Gen Xs' can understand intuitively the motivations of 'Gen Ys' or 'Millennials' is made difficult (where age gaps exist) through AM prior conditioning and experience. Thus, separation might exist between the way in which AMs perceive that their charges should behave and how they actually do – leading to frustration and a lack of engagement. In addition, where AMs are insufficiently attuned to the demographic profile of their customers (whether in terms of socio-economic grouping, age or class etc.) problems can arise: first, by AMs making inappropriate unit-manager selection decisions; and second, in situations where they are permitted some latitude, through the choice of inappropriate product, pricing and promotions strategies.

  - *Cultural distance*: In international IMUEs, in particular, 'values dissonance' can arise between 'host country' AMs and their parent companies. Due to socialisation in their own societal contexts, AMs might find it difficult – privately at least – to accept or enact values that run contrary to those that have been imprinted from childhood. Values such as truth, honesty and integrity might be challenged by notions of creating strong relational ties through favours or gifting, 'saving face' through lies or deception, and covering up misdemeanours to protect immediate colleagues, friends or family. Also, management practices that are taken as standard practice in developed markets (such as participation, open communications, appraisals and empowerment) might be baulked at in territories where self-protective leaders are the sole decision makers, communications are conducted only on a need-to-know basis, honest feedback is rarely given due to the need for both parties to 'save face' and responsibility/accountability is shunned due to a fear of retribution should things go awry.

- **Functional Distance**: In addition to structural and psychological forms of distance, the AM also experiences functional distance which expresses itself in forms of 'outgroup' and vocational separation.

  - *'Outgroup' distance*: The phenomenon of 'outgroup' detachment is connected to hierarchical distance, outlined above. That is to say, as part of the 'ingroup' operational line, AMs invariably struggle to have any affinity or empathy with functional 'outgroups' within the organisation such as HR, finance, marketing and property. Such functions are often regarded as 'getting in the way' because they 'don't actually understand how it's done'. Hostility is often demonstrated and expressed at regional meetings, where AMs openly challenge (or deride) poorly conceived 'initiatives' from central functionaries that are (in their view) clearly separated from the needs and realities of the operational line.

  - *Vocational distance*: Many ex-unit managers who 'transition' into the AM role face a form of vocational disjuncture which is usually expressed as a gap in their understanding of how to 'manage at a distance'. In actual fact, what they really lack is an understanding and appreciation of the vocational and practice-based requirements of being an AM. Thus, whilst they have an intimate appreciation of technical and behavioural aspects of 'hands on' unit supervision, they are deficient with regards to the vocational elements of the job, namely: the technical, behavioural and cognitive skills associated with optimising performance without exercising direct day-to-day control. These problems are exacerbated for graduates directly appointed into the role and techno-crats/support staff parachuted into the job without any prior operational line experience (who, early on as AMs, generally over-index on applying their legacy skill sets).

For all 'transitional' appointees and seasoned AMs, however, there also exists a universal problem relating to vocational understanding down the line, particularly after periods of practice/process changes involving new machinery, product and technology. How can AMs be expected to oversee and supervise others, ensuring that they effectively execute their duties and responsibilities, when – due to their detachment from day-to-day unit operations – AMs have limited knowl-edge of the systems and processes themselves?

To some extent, the issue of distance might be overplayed, given that – on the positive side – unit separation for AMs reduces overfamiliarity (which in its extreme form can reduce respect) and creates an 'allure' which can sustain a high degree of influence. Also, given the lack of time AMs can devote to units, they can concentrate on 'short and sharp' deep-dive 'visits with a purpose' that will not be degraded by procrastination and time wasting. Nevertheless, the issue of distance – in all of its structural, psychological and functional dimensions – poses particular problems for AMs in their effective execution of the role. How, given the distance-related challenges they face, can they expedite successfully the requirements and expectations of their line manager and the wider organisation?

AM PRACTICE–DISTANCE 'FIT' (PDF)

What do effective AMs do to close down the elements of structural, psychological and functional distance referred to above? Whilst answers are provided in chapters 3 to 6, it is pertinent at this point to classify the AM practices which ameliorate each variant of distance. The figure below provides such a classification, juxtaposing distance typologies against the appropriate AM practice-based responses:

Distance Typology SD*	Commitment	AM Practices Control	Change
Physical	Recognition	Delegation	Leads/Champions
Hierarchical	Local Vision	Output Prioritisation	Patch Ups
PD*			
Demographic	Talent 'Fit'	Autonomy	Adjust Mindsets
Cultural	Service Training	Values	Benefit Upselling
FD*			
'Outgroup'	Team Building	Networking	Knowledge Diff.
Vocational	'Train the Trainer'	Blueprint Monitoring	CPI

(*SD: Structural Distance, PD: Psychological Distance, FD: Functional Distance)

Figure 8.1 AM Practice–distance 'Fit' (PDF)

What this table seeks to illustrate is that effective AMs – whether intentionally or not – attempt to solve the multiple problems posed by the different variants of distance by judicious practice applications that enable them to *lead their portfolios without direct daily supervision*. The main facets of commitment, control and change-based practices that help 'reduce' multi-faceted distance issues are:

- **'Reducing' Structural Distance**
  - **Physical distance**
    - *Recognition*: Patronage, public praise, awards and treats which decrease 'spatial detachment' from portfolio goals and objectives
    - *Delegation*: Practical architecture (clusters, families and hub & spoke) that reduce geographical spans of control, increasing 'capacity' and 'bandwidth' for AMs to concentrate on value-added activities (such as selection and talent development)
    - *Leads/champions*: Devolvement of responsibility for processes and initiatives to increase responsibility/ accountability and buy-in at a local level
  - **Hierarchical distance**
    - *Local vision*: Corporate vision/mission/tactics made locally

relevant to increase alignment and reduce 'organisational dissonance'

- *Output prioritisation*: Organisational KPIs and objectives are prioritised to reduce central 'metric overload' and increase local clarity of purpose
- *Patch ups*: Change initiatives are adjusted/amended for local relevance

- **'Reducing' Psychological distance**
  - **Demographic distance**
    - *Talent fit*: GM profile matched to customer demographic to reduce dissonance
    - *Autonomy*: 'Freedom within a frame' to encourage self-expression, enhancing corporate attachment (especially within Gen Y workers)
    - *Adjusting mindsets*: Explanation of the 'why' of change to workers who – due to access to digital communications – are more savvy, thereby increasing alignment
  - **Cultural distance**
    - *Service training*: Service skills development to ensure service-provider behaviour fits the service concept and customer segmentation
    - *Values*: Model/live values so they encourage intentional/purposeful behaviours in conformance with 'distant' corporate norms
    - *Benefit upselling*: Express corporate change in local 'benefits–costs=outcomes' terms to increase buy-in and reduce resistance/sabotage

- **'Reducing' Functional Distance**
  - **'Outgroup' distance**
    - *Trust*: 'Protection from punishment' for followers from non-compliance to rules that are set by functionaries (potentially) detached from the realities of day-to-day operations
    - *Networking*: Increase support staff proximity and levels of internal service through cultivating social connections and relationships
    - *Knowledge diffusion*: Creation of closer internal alliances with 'outgroups' by uncovering/sharing 'hidden value'

- **Vocational distance**
    - *Development*: 'Train the trainers' to enhance operational knowledge and get 'closer to the detail'
    - *Blueprint monitoring*: Regular audits and checks to increase understanding of 'operational minutiae'
    - *CPI*: Relentless process improvement, reducing detachment/improving vocational insight

ARGUMENTS AND CONTRIBUTIONS

As stated, previous scholarship within the multi-unit domain has analysed what AMs do (predominantly in US fast-food contexts) without considering how – in addition to my previous observations on 'practices as a form of social exchange' (Edger 2012) – their practice applications are a conscious/unconscious attempt to mitigate the effects of the multi-faceted problem of distance.

But what are the main insights/arguments of this book and what principal contributions do they make?

- MUEs and reducing 'centre–unit' distance:
    - Organisational level: As Chapter 2 demonstrated, MUEs can alleviate some of the problems faced by AMs by addressing *structural* breakdowns through strategy (i.e. goals that create clear alignment), *psychological* detachment through culture/HRM (i.e. engagement interventions) and *functional* dissonance through robust architecture (i.e. 'flight controllers' and filters).
    - AM role: The beginning of Chapter 3 outlined how MUEs specify what the AM role entails (both in terms of duties and targets) and its resource requirements. In an ideal world, AMs will have access to the information and support they need – in a clear/unambiguous form – so that they have the *capacity* to close down the level of distance between them and their units, becoming archetypal 'proximal leaders' who can fulfil added value development, coaching and knowledge transference/best practice roles. For instance, compliance/auditing/policing duties are made simple by the presence of excellent systems (such as unit 'dashboard' information) that 'free up' the AM to improve service and grow sales.

- AM context, practice responses and distance 'fit':
  - Context: As the end of Chapter 3 highlighted, empirical research indicates that – in many instances – AMs are faced with a number of roadblocks that limit the amount of interactions they have with their followers (both in terms of frequency and positivity!).
  - Practices: Chapters 4–6 showcased a number of practices (commitment, control and change) that have the conscious/unconscious by-product of mitigating or reducing levels of structural, psychological and functional distance in an AM's portfolio. By effecting these techniques, AMs stand a better chance of achieving a 'high level of unit performance without direct supervision'.
  - Practice–distance fit: The 'AM Practice–distance "Fit"' section of this chapter proposes that AMs should deploy certain practices to counter the effects of various distance typologies. This is a novel attempt to reclassify what effective AMs do and for what reason.
- AM personal characteristics:
  - Attribute–distance fit: Chapter 7 highlighted the five main attributes of effective AMs. As some of these practices are associated with specific distance typologies which are clustered within various personal characteristics, it stands to reason that certain attributes have an impact on ameliorating certain categorisations of distance. Hence *expertise* in delegation, prioritising and organising is connected to reducing *structural* distance; *emotional intelligence* with regards to follower exchange deployment is associated with minimising psychological distance; and *entrepreneurship* in relation to stimulating knowledge creation/transference is associated with collapsing levels of functional distance.

FURTHER RESEARCH

This book has attempted to unpack the professional practices of effective AMs and the degree to which these practices might be reframed as having a contingent effect on reducing an AM's level of distance with multiple stakeholders within their MUE. The author admits there are numerous imperfections attached to this study. First, some of the data for this enquiry was derived from previous endeavours into defining effective multi-unit leadership (Edger 2012, 2013) which were not exclusively 'trained upon' the distance problematic. Second, some of the constructs, connections and associations made within this book need further proof-testing and validation. Readers should be confident that the practices and personal characteristics of effective AMs described in this book have received extremely positive reviews from practitioners (indeed, much of the content is used by some major UK MUEs to train and develop their AMs). However, the author accepts that at times – particularly in the chapter summaries and this conclusion – the levels of academic abstraction (linking distance typologies to practices and personal attributes) can seem somewhat complex and off putting. Although I acknowledge that this can be difficult for readers (sitting, as it does, alongside pithy 'how to' lists, questions and illuminating case studies), I am loathe to apologise for at least attempting to expand the 'frontiers of enquiry' in this field beyond erudite simplicity!

Antonakis, J., and Atwater, L. (2002) Leader Distance: A review and a proposed theory. *Leadership Quarterly* 13, 673–704.

Batrus Hollweg International [BHI] (2005a, April 7) Tackling the multi-unit manager challenge, Part 1. *Peak Performance Update.* Available from: http:/www.batrushollweg.com/files/4-7-05.newsletter.MUM1.pdf.

Batrus Hollweg International [BHI] (2005b, April 7) Tackling the multi-unit manager challenge, Part 2. *Peak Performance Update.* Available from: http:/www.batrushollweg.com/files/4-24-05.newsletter.MUM_2.pdf.

Bligh, M., and Riggio, R (eds) (2013) *Exploring Distance in Leader–Follower Relationships: When Near is Far and Far is Near.* New York: Routledge.

Brzezicki, M. (2008) *Examining the Competencies Required to be a Successful Multi-unit Manager*, unpublished PhD dissertation defence, North Central University.

Chang, M-H., and Harrington, J. (2000) Centralization vs. Decentralisation in a Multi-Unit Organization: A Computational Model of a Retail Chain as a Multi-Agent Adaptive System. *Management Science* 46 (11), 1,427–40.

Chase, W.E., and Simon, H.A. (1973) Perception in Chess. *Cognitive Psychology* 4, 55–81.

Child, J. (1988) *Organization: A Guide to Problems and Practice* (2nd edition). London: Paul Chapman.

Collinson, D. (2005) Questions of Distance. *Leadership* 1 (2), 235–50.

Corace, C. (2007) Engagement – Enrolling the quiet majority. *Organization Development Journal* 25 (2), 171–175.

Crainer, S. (1998) *Key Management Ideas: Thinkers that Changed the Management World* (3rd edition). London: Prentice Hall.

DiPietro, R.B., Murphy, K.S., Rivera, M., and Muller, C.C. (2007) Multi-unit management key success factors in the casual dining restaurant industry: a case study. *International Journal of Contemporary Hospitality Management* 19 (7), 524–36.

Drucker, P.F. (1989) *The Practice of Management* (9th edition). London: Heinemann Professional.

Edger, C. (2012) *Effective Multi-Unit Leadership – Local Leadership in Multi-Site Situations*. Aldershot: Gower.

Edger, C. (2013) *International Multi-Unit Leadership – Developing Local Leaders in International Multi-Site Operations*. Aldershot: Gower.

Ericsson, K.A. (2000) *Expert Performance and Deliberate Practice*. Available at: http://www.psy.fsu.edu/faculty/ericsson/ericsson.exp.perf.html [accessed 21 June 2011].

Fox, C. (2014) Exploring Personal Characteristics in the Multi-Unit Leader Role and the Effect of Structural Distance in the Leader-Follower Relationship. Unpublished MSc dissertation, Birmingham City University.

Garvin, D.A., and Levesque, L.C. (2008) The Multi-Unit Enterprise. *Harvard Business Review* June, 1–11.

Gladwell, M. (2008) *Outliers: The Story of Success.* New York: Little, Brown and Co.

Goldman, A.I. (1999) *Knowledge in a Social World.* Oxford: Oxford University Press.

Goleman, D. (1998) *Working with Emotional Intelligence.* New York: Bantam Books.

Guest, D. (1997) Human Resource Management and Performance: A Review and Research Agenda. *International Journal of HRM* 8, 263–76.

Hamel, G. (2000) Waking Up IBM: How a gang of Unlikely Rebels Transformed Big Blue. *Harvard Business Review* July–August, 137–144.

Harrison, R. (1972) How to Describe Your Organization's Culture. *Harvard Business Review* May–June, 119–28.

Hofstede, G. (1980) *Culture's Consequences: International Differences in Work-Related Values*. Beverley Hills, CA: Sage.

Hofstede, G. (1991) *Cultures and Organisations*. London: McGraw Hill.

House, R., Hanges, P., Javidan, M., Dorfman, P., and Gupta, V. (2004) *Culture, Leadership and Organization: The GLOBE Study of 62 Societies*. Thousand Oaks, CA: Sage.

Jaeger, A. (1983) The transfer of organizational culture overseas: An approach to control in the multinational corporation. *Journal of International Business Studies* 14(2): 91–114.

Janis, I. (1972) *Victims of Groupthink.* Boston, MA: Houghton Mifflin.

Jeffreys, J.B. (1954) *Retail Trading in Britain 1850–1950.* Cambridge: Cambridge University Press.

Johnston, R., and Clark, G. (2008) *Services Operations Management – Improving Service Delivery.* London: Pearson.

Jones, P., and Inkinci, Y. (2001) *An analysis of multi-unit management in UK restaurant chains*. Proceedings from the 2001 CAUTHE National Research Conference, Queensland, Australia: Council for Australian University Tourism & Hospitality Education.

Kotter, J.P., and Cohen, D.S. (2002) *The Heart of Change*. Boston, MA: Harvard Business School Press.

Lawler, E.E. (1976) Control Systems in Organizations. In M.D. Dunnette (ed.), *Handbook of Industrial and Organizational Psychology*. New York: Rand McNally.

Lewin, K. (1951) *Field Theory in Social Science*. New York: Harper and Row.

Mathias, P. (1967) *Retailing Revolution: A History of Multiple Retailing in the Food Trades Based upon the Allied Suppliers Group of Companies*. London: Europa Publications.

May, D., Gilson, R., and Harter, L. (2004) The psychological conditions of meaningfulness, safety and availability and the engagement of human spirit at work. *Journal of Occupational and Organizational Psychology* 77 (1), 11–37.

Meyer, J.P., and Allen, N.J. (1991) A three-component conceptualization of organizational commitment: Some methodological considerations. *Human Resource Management Review* 1, 61–98.

Mintzberg, H. (1979) *The Structuring of Organisations*. New York: Prentice Hall.

Mintzberg, H. (2009) *Managing*. London: Pearson

Mone, M.A., and Umbreit, W.T. (1989) Making the transition from single-unit to multi-unit fast-service management: what are the requisite skills and educational needs? *Journal of Hospitality and Tourism Research* 13 (3), 319–31.

Muller, C.C., and Campbell, D.F. (1995) The attributes and attitudes of multi-unit managers in a national quick-service restaurant firm. *Journal of Hospitality and Tourism Research* 19 (2), 3–18.

Napier, B., and Ferris, G. (1993) Distance in Organisations. *Human Resource Management Review* 3, 321–57.

Nonaka, I., and Takeuchi, H. (1995) *The Knowledge Creating Company*. New York: Oxford University Press.

Olsen, M.D., Tse, E.C., and West, J.J. (1992) *Strategic Management in the Hospitality Industry*. New York: Van Nostrand Reinhold.

Ouchi, W. (1979) A conceptual framework for the design of organizational control mechanisms. *Management Science* 25(9): 833.

Park, R. (1924) The concept of social distance as applied to the study of racial attitudes and racial relations. *Journal of Applied Sociology* 8, 339–44.

Poole, W. (1927) Distance in Sociology. *The American Journal of Sociology* 33, 94–104.

Reis, D., and Pena, L. (2001) Reengineering the Motivation to Work. *Management Decision* 39 (8), 666–75.

Reynolds, D. (2000) An exploratory investigation into behaviorally based success characteristics of foodservice managers. *Journal of Hospitality and Tourism Research* 24 (1), 92–103.

Reynolds, J., Howard, E., Cuthbertson, C., and Hristov, L. (2007) Perspectives on Retail Format Innovation: Relating Theory and Practice. *International Journal of Retail and Distribution Management* 35 (8), 647–60.

Ritzer, G. (1993) *The McDonaldization of Society.* Thousand Oaks, CA: Sage.

Rivera, M., Di Pietro, R.B., Murphy, K.S., and Muller, C.C. (2008) Multi-unit managers: training needs and competencies for casual dining restaurants. *International Journal of Contemporary Hospitality Management* 20 (6), 616–30.

Rummel, R. (1976) *The Conflict Helix: Vol. 2: Understanding Conflict and War.* Beverly Hills, CA: Sage.

Ryan, W.E. (1992) *Identification and comparison of management skills required for single and multi-unit management in independently operated college and university food services*, unpublished doctoral dissertation, Oklahoma State University, Stillwater.

Scarborough, J. (1998) Comparing Chinese and Western cultural roots: Why 'east is east' and... *Business Horizons*, November–December, 15–24.

Schmenner, R. (1986) How are service businesses to survive and prosper? *Sloan Management Review.* Spring, 21–32.

Schwartz, I. (2007) Manage Your Energy, Not Your Time. *Harvard Business Review* October, 63–73.

Schyns, B. (2013) The Role of Distance in Leader–Member Exchange. In *Exploring Distance in Leader–Follower Relationships: When Near is Far and Far is Near*, M. Bligh and R. Riggio (eds), 136–54.

Shamir, B. (1995) Social Distance and charisma: Theoretical notes and an exploratory study. *Leadership Quarterly* 6, 19–47.

Shirom, A. (2006) Explaining vigor: On the antecedents and consequences of vigor as a positive affect at work. In C. Cooper and

D. Nelson (eds), *Organizational Behaviour: Accentuating the positive at work*. Thousand Oaks, CA: Sage.

Simmel, G. (1908) *Socziologie: Untersuchungen uber die formen der vergesellscaftung*. Berlin: Duncker and Humblot. Levine, D. translation.

Slack, N., Chambers, S., Johnston, R., and Betts, A. (2009) *Operations and Process Management – Principles and Practice for Strategic Intent.* London: Pearson.

Tannenbaum, A.S. (1968) *Control in Organizations.* New York: McGraw-Hill.

Toffler, A. (1970) *Future Shock.* New York: Pan Books.

Umbreit, W.T. (1989) Multi-unit management: managing at a distance. *Cornell Hotel and Restaurant Administration Quarterly* 30 (1), 52–9.

Umbreit, W.T., and Smith, D.I. (1991) A study of the opinions and practices of successful multi-unit fast service restaurant managers. *Hospitality Research Journal* 14, 451–8.

Volberda, H., Baden-Fuller, C., and van den Bosch, F. (2001) Mastering Strategic Renewal: Mobilising Renewal Journeys in Multi-Unit Firms. *Long Range Planning* 34, 159–178.

Zhu, W., Avolio, B., and Walumbwa, F. (2009) Moderating role of follower characteristics with transformational leadership and follower work engagement. *Group and Organization Management* 34 (5), 590–619.